THE LITTLE BOOK OF BRIDGERTON

THE LITTLE BOOK OF BRIDGERTON

The Regency World of Bridgerton
Laid Bare

Charlotte Browne

BLINK
bringing you closer

First published in the UK by Blink Publishing
An imprint of Bonnier Books UK
3.08, The Plaza, 535 King's Road, Chelsea, London SW10 0SZ
Owned by Bonnier Books
Sveavägen 56, Stockholm, Sweden

www.blinkpublishing.co.uk

facebook.com/blinkpublishing
twitter.com/blinkpublishing

Hardback – 978-1-788-704-70-0
eBook – 978-1-788-704-71-7

A CIP catalogue of this book is available from the British Library.

Typeset by IDSUK (DataConnection) Ltd
Printed and bound in Great Britain by Clays Ltd, Elcograf S.p.A.

1 3 5 7 9 10 8 6 4 2

Every reasonable effort has been made to trace copyright holders of material
reproduced in this book, but if any have been inadvertently overlooked the
publishers would be glad to hear from them.

Blink Publishing is an imprint of Bonnier Books UK
www.bonnierbooks.co.uk

Contents

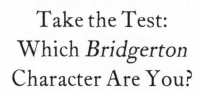

Take the Test:
Which *Bridgerton*
Character Are You?

1. You've received an invite to a ball. What's your first thought?
   a) It's an opportunity to find true love
   b) Time to leave the country again
   c) Repel every ambitious mama in the room
   d) How do I get out of this tedious, torrid ordeal?
   e) It's an opportunity to concoct witty observations from the side-lines

2. What's your most favourite accessory?
   a) Anything, so long as it's blue and discreet
   b) A green and understated brooch
   c) An antique watch

    d) I don't care for accessories, I'd rather have a book in my hand

    e) A bright yellow parasol

3. How would you describe your hairstyle?

    a) Swept up with an Audrey Hepburn-inspired fringe

    b) Thick, luscious and gleaming, with a little stubble at the sides

    c) Channelling Grecian god vibes, with my thick, luscious locks and sideburns

    d) I prefer to simply stick a ribbon round my head rather than waste time faffing about with my locks

    e) Elaborate and a little ostentatious, I'd be lost without my curling irons and pomade

4. What do you look for in a partner?

    a) Passion, a good sense of humour and an adventurous spirit for the outdoors

    b) Someone who won't mind me slobbering all over the silver cutlery

    c) Status and money, but will turn a blind eye to my mistress on the side

d) Someone I can share a cigarette and intellectual conversation with
e) A heart of gold, someone who's always got my back and loves me for who I am

5. How do you alleviate a bad mood?
   a) Hammer out Beethoven on my pianoforte
   b) Punch the living daylights out of a boxing bag in the gym
   c) Randomly declare a duel at dawn or settle for clay pigeon shooting
   d) Dig out my trusty copy of *A Vindication of the Rights of Woman* to remind me just how far the fairer sex has come
   e) Unleash a set of barbed and wickedly wry observations upon my adversaries on Twitter

6. What's your favourite hobby?
   a) Spending quality time with loved ones and family
   b) Riding gallantly down a cobbled street, atop a fine stallion
   c) Sitting in the window of White's appraising the other dandies strutting past

d) Reading, reading and more reading

e) Sorting out everybody else's business

7. What song will get you up on the dancefloor?
   a) Taylor Swift – 'Wildest Dreams'
   b) Sister Sledge – 'He's the Greatest Dancer'
   c) LMFAO – 'Sexy and I Know It'
   d) Billie Eilish – 'Bad Guy'
   e) Ed Sheeran – 'Perfect'

8. What's your greatest ambition?
   a) Set up an enormous soft play centre for all the children in the surrounding villages so I'm surrounded by as many of the little darlings as possible
   b) Open up my own Regency-themed Center Parcs, complete with riding, shooting, fishing and boxing facilities. Breeches and hussar boots mandatory attire
   c) Design my own dandy-inspired clothing range complete with customised embroidered three-piece suits and stylish linen neckerchiefs
   d) Organise ladies-only retreats, where women receive weapon and combat training inspired

by the Ancient Amazonians. All topped off with a roundup of the best feminist literature before bedtime

e) Become a top TV presenter who is highly skilled in the art of manipulating information out of celebrities and politicians, revealing them for the true hypocrites and vain, glorified idiots that they are!

9. How would others describe you?
   a) Sweet, kind and virtuous, I'm never one to commit a fashion blunder
   b) Suave, aloof, a little frosty and mysterious
   c) A good sport who cares about his family but is prone to obnoxious outbursts
   d) Vivacious, opinionated and ready with a quick-witted putdown
   e) The friend that everyone can truly depend on

Mostly As: Daphne

A paragon of virtue, you mostly float through life looking wonderful and being marvellous.

Mostly Bs: Simon

Cool, calm and collected, you excel at most sports and outdoor activities. Your unruffled demeanour is only agitated when exposed to a prolonged and uncomfortable burning sensation.

Mostly Cs: Anthony

No one can deny you've got style effortlessly nailed but it might be wise to spend a little less time coiffing your hair in front of the mirror each day if you want to find a genuine relationship.

Mostly Ds: Eloise

You're a force to be reckoned with, who regularly defies conventions and questions the established order.

Mostly Es: Penelope

There's a lot more to you than meets the eye. Though consistently kind and loyal, you're not somebody anyone would like to get on the wrong side of.

Chapter 1
A Regency Timeline

The strict definition of the Regency period covers 1811–20. In those nine years, George, Prince Regent ruled in place of his father, George III, who was declared mentally unfit to rule the country in the last decade of his reign after regular bouts of severe illness. But the Regency era has come to represent a much wider period of time, defined and characterised by huge social, cultural and economic changes. Most historians agree that this tumultuous time began around the latter years of George III's reign in the 1790s and ended with the death of his second son, William IV, in 1837. The Regency period continues to fascinate and excite us to this day. From the Battle of Trafalgar to the construction of the Royal Pavilion at Brighton and the publication of Jane

Austen's *Pride and Prejudice*, what were the events and culturally significant moments that marked this extraordinary era?

1790

The young painter Thomas Lawrence receives his first royal commission, a portrait of Queen Charlotte. He would go on to become the country's leading portrait painter, painting some of the most celebrated and famous figures of the day.

Child prodigy Joseph Turner is accepted into the Royal Academy of Arts at the tender age of 14.

Mozart's opera in two acts, *Cosi fan Tutte*, premieres in Vienna.

The Oxford Canal is opened. For 15 years, it carried coal and agricultural products between the Midlands and London.

1791

William Wilberforce introduces the first Parliamentary bill to abolish the slave trade but it is rejected.

The Society of United Irishmen is formed, to unite Protestants and Catholics, in the wake of the French Revolution.

1792

Mary Wollstonecraft publishes the groundbreaking *A Vindication of the Rights of Women*, the first book to argue for the equality of men and women. Whig politician Horace Walpole describes her as 'a hyena in petticoats'.

France is declared a republic.

1793

King Louis XVI and Queen Marie Antoinette are found guilty of treason by the National Convention and executed at the guillotine.

Scottish explorer Alexander Mackenzie becomes the first person to complete a transcontinental crossing of North America.

1795

Prime Minister William Pitt introduces bills that forbid large meetings and political lectures. It becomes an act of treason to incite hatred against the King or his government.

George, Prince of Wales, marries Princess Caroline of Brunswick-Wolfenbüttel. It was an arranged marriage and the pair took an instant dislike to each other. Upon meeting, he called for a glass of brandy and she is reported to have said: 'He's very fat and nothing like as handsome as his portrait.'

Riots break out across towns in Britain due to high prices and a shortage of bread.

Ludwig van Beethoven makes his long-awaited public debut in Vienna with a performance of one of his own piano concertos.

1796

Edward Jenner develops the first successful vaccine against smallpox.

Princess Charlotte is born at Carlton House to George, Prince of Wales, and Princess Caroline.

1797

Haberdasher John Hetherington is arrested for disturbing the peace after he leaves his shop in the Strand, London, wearing a silk top hat. He is charged for wearing a 'tall structure having a shiny luster calculated to frighten timid people'. Not long after, he is inundated with orders.

Samuel Taylor Coleridge writes the poem 'Kubla Khan' after a dream under the influence of opium.

1800

Napoleon Bonaparte crosses the Alps with his army and invades northern Italy.

1801

The Parliaments of Great Britain and Ireland unite in the Act of Union. The Union Jack becomes the new flag of the United Kingdom.

1802

The Treaty of Amiens temporarily ends hostilities between France and the UK.

The Factory Act is passed by Parliament to regulate conditions in the cotton mills.

The Rosetta Stone – which provides the key to understanding ancient hieroglyphics – goes on display at the British Museum for the first time. It remains there to this day.

French founder Madame Marie Tussaud arrives in London to exhibit her wax figures for the first time at the Lyceum Theatre.

1803

Napoleon Bonaparte sells all the French territories to the United States in a bid to prepare for an invasion of England. Britain declares war on France and begins to fortify the coast of southeast England. The country lives under constant threat of invasion.

1804

Napoleon is crowned Emperor of France. In protest, Beethoven renames his Third Symphony from *Napoleon* to *Eroica*.

Spain declares war on Britain.

Thomas Lawrence paints a portrait of Princess Caroline of Brunswick. The two are alleged to have grown close during her sittings and the propriety of their relationship was called into question.

1805

The British Royal Navy defeats the French and Spanish fleet at the Battle of Trafalgar. The most important battle of the Napoleonic Wars, their victory ensured that Napoleon would never invade Britain. Joseph Turner was commissioned by the royal family to paint *The Battle of Trafalgar* as a tribute to national hero Admiral Horatio Nelson, who died in the battle.

1806

Lord Nelson is the first commoner to be given a state funeral. 'In one of the greatest Aquatic Processions that ever was beheld on the River Thames' his coffin was carried from Greenwich to Whitehall Stairs.

Napoleon enforces a blockade that forbids every major power in Europe from trading with Britain. His plan was to destroy the country through economic warfare but it encouraged British merchants to seek out new markets and expand their trade with the rest of the world.

The British women's magazine *La Belle Assemblée* is published for the first time. Its beautiful engravings and fashion prints have proved to be a fantastic resource for Regency historians.

1807

The Slave Trade Act is passed in the House of Lords, prohibiting the slave trade in the British Empire. However, slavery still remained legal in most of the Empire until the Slavery Abolition Act of 1833.

Gas lighting is installed in Pall Mall, London. It was the first street anywhere to be illuminated by gaslight.

Napoleon invades Spain.

William Wordsworth publishes two volumes of poetry that include 'I Wandered Lonely as a Cloud' and 'The World Is Too Much With Us'.

The Parthenon Marbles (also known as the Elgin Marbles), originally part of the temple of the Parthenon, are put on display at the British Museum. The poet Lord Byron decries the acquisition of the relics as an act of theft.

1808

The Peninsular War, an important phase of the Napoleonic Wars, begins. English lawyer Henry Crabb Robinson becomes the world's first war correspondent when he sends his reports on the conflict in Spain to *The Times* in London.

Humphry Davy publicly demonstrates in London that electricity can produce heat or light between two electrodes. People are astonished by this revelation and several women in the audience swoon.

1809

Arthur Wellesley (later 1st Duke of Wellington) joins forces with the Spanish Army at the Battle of Talavera. They defeat the French and Wellesley returns to Britain a hero. Not long after, he is appointed Baron Douro and Viscount Wellington.

Jenny Pipes of Leominster becomes the last woman to suffer the ducking stool as punishment for being a common scold – i.e. a woman causing a public disturbance.

The Conservative politician George Canning plots to have War Minister Viscount Castlereagh removed. When Castlereagh uncovers his plan, he challenges Canning to a duel on Putney Heath. Although both miss on their first shot, Castlereagh manages to strike Canning in the thigh on his second attempt. After he helps the injured Canning limp away, the two are soon back on civil terms.

1810

George III is declared insane after the death of his daughter Princess Amelia sends him into another serious bout of mental illness.

Walter Scott publishes 'The Lady of the Lake', a poem in six cantos. A runaway success, it sold 25,000 copies.

Lord Byron swims across the Hellespont, a tumultuous Turkish strait now known as the Dardanelles, in imitation of the mythical protagonist Leander, who swam the passage each night to be with his lover, Hero.

The Spanish artist Francisco Goya begins 'The Disasters of War' series of 82 etchings.

Napoleon marries by proxy Archduchess Marie Louise of Austria after he annuls his marriage to Josephine, who has not produced an heir.

1811

George, Prince of Wales, becomes Regent at the beginning of the year. That summer, he holds an extremely lavish fête at his residence Carlton House. Two thousand guests attend the most prestigious event of the year and no expense is spared – one of the most extraordinary features is a 200-foot table with gold and silver coloured fish swimming through a canal of water in the centre. Queen Charlotte refuses to attend or to let her daughters go as she is angry at her son for celebrating while his father, George III, is ill.

Textile workers, who become known as 'Luddites', destroy machinery in the Midlands, in protest that they are being put out of work. Their actions spark a movement that spreads throughout England.

London's population passes the one million mark.

British architect John Nash begins building Regent Street in collaboration with James Burton as part of his development of the West End of London.

Jane Austen's *Sense and Sensibility* is published anonymously.

Mary Anning, aged 12, discovers a 30-foot-long fossil in Lyme Regis, Dorset. She goes on to become a palaeontologist, who contributes greatly to the science of prehistoric life.

1812

America declares war on Britain over trade restrictions with France and forced recruitment of US seamen into the Royal Navy.

Spencer Perceval becomes the only British prime minister to date to have been assassinated. He dies at the hands of a merchant with a grievance against his government.

London's main streets are lit by gas.

The waltz makes its debut in London's ballrooms.

Lord Byron's *Childe Harold's Pilgrimage*, a narrative poem in four parts, is published. Based on his travels around the Mediterranean, it propels him into the bigtime.

Napoleon invades Russia in June. The French Army fail to conquer the country and make their retreat four months later.

The Brothers Grimm publish their first collection of fairy tales.

1813

The Luddite movement (a movement away from modern technology and machinery, which workers believed threatened their jobs) is quashed when 17 of its leaders are hanged.

King of the dandies Beau Brummell snubs the Prince Regent when he asks Lord Alvanley: 'Alvanley, who is your fat friend?' The two, once close friends, never speak again.

The journalist Leigh Hunt is imprisoned for libel after criticising the Prince Regent, the future King George IV, in the Radical paper *The Examiner*.

The Royal Philharmonic Society of London is founded.

Wellington defeats Napoleon's forces at the Battle of Vitoria.

Jane Austen's *Pride and Prejudice*, a novel of manners, is published.

1814

During an extreme winter the Thames freezes over. City dwellers flock there over four days for an impromptu Frost Fair, where they enjoy gingerbread, roast oxen and sip gin. The ice is so thick, an elephant is marched along the river. It is to be the last ever Frost Fair.

Napoleon abdicates and is exiled to the island of Elba.

Wellington is made a Duke and the Regent holds a fête in his honour at Carlton House.

Britain and America sign a peace treaty.

George Stephenson tests his first working steam locomotive, *Blucher* (named after Gebhard Leberecht von Blücher, the Prussian general).

Lord Byron publishes *The Corsair*. The tale in verse sells 10,000 copies on the first day.

1815

In February, Napoleon escapes from Elba and arrives in France. In March, an alliance is formed between Britain, Prussia, Russia and Austria to fight against him. Three months later, Wellington's army defeats

Napoleon once and for all at the Battle of Waterloo. Napoleon is banished to St Helena in the October.

John Nash begins the reconstruction of the Royal Pavilion in Brighton. He replaces the neoclassical pavilion with minarets and domes.

The painter Thomas Lawrence is knighted by the Regent.

John Loudon McAdam invents a new method for surfacing roads. The 'macadamisation' was to revolutionise travel.

1816

The Regent and Princess Caroline's only daughter Princess Charlotte marries Prince Leopold of Saxe-Coburg.

Radicals call two mass public meetings at Spa Fields in Islington, London, to demand electoral and land reforms. The first ends peacefully but the second descends into riots.

After accruing huge debts, Beau Brummell flees England for France. He never returns.

Lord Byron's wife Anne Milbanke leaves him. Dogged by scandalous rumours involving adultery, marital violence and incest, Byron leaves England, never to return.

Mary Godwin, the daughter of Mary Wollstonecraft, marries poet Percy Bysshe Shelley. That same year, she goes on to write the classic Gothic novel, *Frankenstein*.

A major volcanic eruption in Indonesia causes temperatures to plummet across the world, creating the 'Year Without a Summer'. It inspires Byron's poem 'Darkness'.

Jane Austen's novel *Emma* is published. She dedicates the lively comedy of manners to the Regent, who was a great admirer of her work. Historians have since interpreted the excessive deference in her dedication to be a mockery of his character.

1817

The Prince Regent is shot at in his carriage as he returns from the opening of Parliament.

Jane Austen dies at the age of 41.

Princess Charlotte dies after delivering a stillborn son.

1818

Twenty-year-old Mary Shelley publishes *Frankenstein*.

Jane Austen's *Northanger Abbey* and *Persuasion* are published together posthumously in a four-volume set.

John Keats' poem *Endymion* is published.

German inventor Karl von Drais develops the first-known two-wheeled vehicle. It has a seat and handlebars, but no pedals.

British obstetrician Dr James Blundell carries out the first blood transfusion using human blood.

1819

Eleven are killed and over 500 injured when cavalry charge a crowd of 60,000 people at a public meeting calling for political reform. Percy Bysshe Shelley writes *The Mask of Anarchy* in protest. It has since been described as 'the greatest political poem ever written in English'.

Parliament passes the Six Acts to suppress any further meetings.

1820

George III dies at Windsor. The Prince Regent is proclaimed King George IV.

A plot to kill British cabinet ministers and overthrow the government is uncovered. It becomes known as the Cato Street Conspiracy. Most of the conspirators are found guilty of treason and executed.

The Regent's Canal opens fully after a decade of construction. It carries 120,000 tons of cargo in its first year.

1821

Napoleon Bonaparte dies, aged 51, on St Helena.

Queen Caroline, estranged wife of King George VI, dies weeks after being refused entry to her husband's coronation.

Pierce Egan's *Life in London* is published. The comical monthly publication detailing high and low life across the capital is a big hit.

1824

Lord Byron dies in Greece. His body is brought back to be buried in Westminster Abbey but this is refused, due to his 'questionable morality'.

1825

The Stockton and Darlington Railway opens to transport coal from the north to the south of the country. It is the first to use steam locomotives to transport passengers on a public railway. Over the years, more branches open and are instrumental in developing new towns.

Beethoven's Ninth Symphony is performed by the Royal Philharmonic Society in the Argyll Rooms in Regent Street, London. It is the first time the seminal work is performed in Britain. The concert hall is no longer there but a plaque in its place commemorates the event.

1830

George IV dies. William IV ascends to the throne at the advanced age of 69.

Chapter 2
Regency Lingo: A Guide

Would your friends describe you as 'something of a bluestocking'? How would you react if a Bond Street beau whispered in your ear that you're 'the prime article'? Would you accept his compliment or assume he's just offering you a 'Spanish coin'?

Does your mother live in eternal fear of you becoming an 'ape-leader'? If any of this sounds like nonsense to you, take some time to swot up on our glossary of cant and common Regency phrases – soon you'll be conversing like a pro with the best of Georgian society!

Ways to Describe a Lady
A bit of muslin – An attractive female.
Abbess – A mistress of the brothel.

Adventuress – Prostitute or loose woman.

> How to use in speech: 'Colin would do well to pick up some cartography tips from a fellow adventuress abroad before he even thinks of finding himself in want of a wife.'

Ape-leader – Less-than-complimentary term for an older single woman or spinster. If you couldn't find yourself a man during your time on earth, you were fated to lead apes in hell.

Bluestocking – An intellectual woman who enjoys reading literature and wants to stimulate her mind. Comes from the 18th-century Blue Stockings Society led by hostess and critic Elizabeth Montagu.

> How to use in speech: 'That bluestocking Eloise would do well to lift her head out of her book for five minutes and take note of the gentlemen callers who may be vying for her attention. Else she'll end up a right old ape-leader!'

Chit – A bawdy, cheeky young girl.

Diamond of the First Water – An extremely beautiful woman.

Haymarket ware – A prostitute.

Jade – A disreputable woman.

> How to use in speech: 'Queen Charlotte didn't wish to see any jades befouling her court.'

Romp – A forward lady.

Ways to Describe a Gentleman

Beau – A male fashion icon, often good-looking but vain.

> How to use in speech: 'That beau is too in love with himself to ever notice you.'

Blade – A younger, more impetuous and rather less refined version of the beau (above).

> How to use in speech: 'Oh my! Look how that dashing blade cuts a fine strut on the dancefloor!'

Buck – Not dissimilar to a rake but one who enjoys sport and pursues fights.

Cicisbeo – A married woman's lover.

Corinthian – A well-rounded gent who is not only well-mannered and well-dressed but also extremely accomplished in the popular sporting activities of the day – fencing, boxing, shooting and riding.

> How to use in speech: 'Every young lady hopes the rake she's fallen for will one day blossom into a Corinthian.'

Johnny raw – Inexperienced young lad.

Loose in the haft – On the rakish side!

Nonesuch or nonpareil – Male equivalent of the 'Diamond of the First Water' – the Duke, basically!

Peep-o-day boy – A young man who engages in pranks or mischief.

Nefarious Activities

Barking irons – pistols.

> How to use in speech: 'Bring me my goddamn barking iron – I duel at dawn!'

Bilk – To cheat.

> How to use in speech: Most likely down the gambling den at White's – 'You treacherous swine, you're trying to bilk me for everything you can get!'

Ivory turned – Someone who cheats in card games.

How to Describe Someone Who's Had Too Much to Drink During a Wild Night Out in White's

In our opinion, these rival 'hammered', 'plastered' and 'steaming'.

- Drunk as a wheelbarrow
- Dipping too deep
- Eaten Hull cheese (from the Hull cheese pub, which was home to some very strong ales)
- Foxed.

It was very rare to see a lady of the ton intoxicated, although they were allowed to get a little 'half-sprung' or 'jug-bitten' – i.e. tipsy.

Insults

A loose fish – A lecherous drunk.

A vulgar mushroom – A pretentious and somewhat vulgar member of the nouveau riche.

How to use in speech: 'Mrs Featherington's garish taste in clothes betrays her as a vulgar mushroom.'

Bacon-faced – Someone with a fat face.

Bear-garden jaw – A person who uses vulgar language.

Buffle-headed or a dunderhead – An idiot.

> How to use in speech: 'Don't be such a dunderhead!'

Cheeseparing – Miserly or mean with money.

Cursed rum touch – Strange person.

Dicked in the nob – Foolish or crazed.

> How to use in speech: 'He'd had so many whiskys in White's by half nine, he was behaving more than a little dicked in the nob.

Half flash – Naive.

High in the instep – Haughty or proud.

Merry Andrew – A fool or buffoon.

> How to use in speech: 'He made a right Merry Andrew of himself when he subjected her to his self-penned sonnet.'

Wet goose – A stupid person.

Expressions

Bone box: Head.

How to use in speech: 'Get that useless rake out of your bone box!'

Bouncer – An outright lie.

How to use in speech: 'He kept up with his bouncers all night.'

Canterbury Tales – A long and boring story.

How to use in speech: 'I got stuck with him telling me a Canterbury tale all night.'

Claptrap – Talking nonsense.
Corky – Lively or animated.
Countenance – A person's facial expression.

How to use in speech: 'Your countenance does not conceal your revulsion for Lord Rutledge, Marina.'

Cut one's eye teeth – To become wise or understand how the world works.
Doing it much too brown – To lie or exaggerate, embellish.
Faradiddles – Foolish or small lies.

Fit of the Blue-devils – Extremely sad and melancholy.

> How to use in speech: 'Poor Daphne is so blue-deviled by the Duke's rejection, she's lost all vigour even for the pianoforte.'

In a dudgeon – To feel angry or in a bad mood.
In high ropes – To feel ecstatic or in high spirits.

> How to use in speech: 'Daphne remains in high ropes, the morning after her wedding night in the coaching inn.'

Make a mull of it – Mess up a situation.
Napping her bib – Weeping to get her own way.
Pitching the gammon – To tell tall stories.
Plant a facer – Punch someone in the face (particularly used in the sport of boxing).

> How to use in speech: 'Damn, Daphne! I've never seen a lady plant a facer like that!'

Set up one's bristles – To irritate or offend someone.
Sprained her ankle – Fallen pregnant.
Swell – A wealthy and pompous person.

Swimming in lard or well-breeched – Wealthy.

The cut – To snub someone.

To cast up one's accounts – To vomit ('Shoot the cat' was also a popular expression).

> How to use in speech: 'He's paying for his overin-dulgence today – I've never seen a man cast up his accounts in such an involuntary fashion!'

To offer a Spanish coin – To flatter with compliments.

> How to use in speech: 'You'll oft find him in the corner of the dancefloor, offering Spanish coins to any nice bit of muslin he can feast his eyes on.'

To swallow one's spleen – To control one's temper.

Love and Marriage

Become a tenant for life – Get married.

Carte-blanche – Financial support often offered to a man's mistress.

Cry-off – Call off the wedding.

Set your cap at a man – Set your sights on a man and set out to win a proposal.

Smelling of April and May – Madly in love.

Money

Haven't a sixpence to scratch with – Completely broke.

Outrun the constable – To overspend or overindulge.

Rhino – Money.

Swallow a spider – Go bankrupt.

Under the hatches or cucumberish – To be in debt.

Chapter 3
Life Skills for the Ton

From working the eye contact to looking approachable and perfecting how to make positive small talk, women's magazines have long been issuing their readers with instructions on how to attract men. The etiquette manuals for society ladies in the Regency era were no different – although they would most certainly have omitted the Duke's top ten tips for solo pleasuring, or how to have a quickie undetected during a boxing match!

As we know from Daphne Bridgerton's story, a woman's virtue was highly prized. Regency society was remarkably fickle and it could take just one small incident for her honour to be called into question. Daphne is perceived as highly desirable at the start of the season, but as Lady Whistledown wryly observes the more a lady dazzles, the faster she may blaze. So, how did a lady of the ton manage to stay at the top of her game and avoid the pitfalls of scandal or ostracisation? What were the behaviours she needed to cultivate and what were the rules – unspoken or not – she must abide by?

Perfecting the Blush

Appearances were everything in the Regency era. Even if a lady's thoughts were as filthy as a Stephenson steam locomotive, it was certainly not permissible for her ever to reveal them. If she was 'quick to blush', men could breathe a sigh of relief. This involuntary reddening of the cheeks was a clear sign that she possessed an innocent mind. A woman wasn't permitted ever to draw attention to herself actively, but if she blushed in response to admiring glances then this also indicated modesty, reserve and humility. In an excerpt from *The Female Instructor*, a conduct manual published around 1811, the author writes:

> When a girl ceases to blush, she has lost the most powerful charm of beauty. That extreme sensibility

which it indicates may be a weakness and incumbrance in our sex, as I have too often felt; but in yours it is peculiarly engaging. Blushing is far from being necessary an attendant to guilt, that it is the usual companion of innocence.

This modesty, which I think so essential in your sex, will naturally dispose you to be rather silent in company, especially in a large one.

Little wonder that Daphne asks her maid, Rose Nolan, to apply more blusher as she prepares all weapons in her arsenal to catch Prince Friedrich of Prussia's eye at the ball. Women who smeared their lips with paint were judged to be vain or eager to draw attention to themselves, a definite no-no. But wearing a little rouge or 'setting a nap on the cheek' – as was the slang of the day – was permissible.

Never Make the First Move

Perhaps not surprisingly for the day, etiquette manuals encouraged women to conceal or suppress their true feelings until the man had properly declared his interest or intentions. Women could alert potential suitors via their friends or family that they were keen, but they would certainly never be forward enough to approach a man directly. To ask him for a dance or even acknowledge him in the street was tantamount to social suicide. Again, the more demure a woman, the more she was equated to modesty and humility. In Dr John Gregory's conduct manual, *A Father's Legacy to his Daughters*, he writes: 'One of the chief beauties in a female character is that modest reserve, that retiring delicacy, which avoids the public eye, and is disconcerted even at the gaze of admiration.' Some went so far as to advise never even looking at a man unless he made the first move.

Penelope Featherington's decision to declare her true feelings to Colin is unusual for a woman from this period but hints at her independent spirit and courage to defy the social conventions of the day. Coquettish behaviour was widely regarded as deplorable, especially if the lady engaged in flirting for sheer fun and without any serious motivation. Manuals of the time also declared that there was no such thing as a 'good-natured kiss' – *The Mirror of Graces* warned that it would end extremely badly for women who engaged in such behaviour. Which begs the question, were there any Regency debutantes who would ever have risked a passionate clinch in a garden maze? Perhaps we'll never know.

With all this protocol to follow, it's perhaps not surprising that fan flirting became so popular!

Be Ladylike At All Times

In the Regency period, it was important for middle- and upper-class women to be educated enough to craft a well-written letter, converse adequately on the topics of the day and read the scriptures, which were considered essential reading for accomplished females. A lady was expected to be a witty conversationalist, though not an intellectual threat to her husband. Young ladies were also expected to be adept at needlework, watercolour painting and the pianoforte – one of the reasons the latter was so popular was that it avoided the potentially unsettling sight of a woman exerting too much physical energy, while blowing into a wind instrument or raising her arms too vigorously to play the violin.

In *Bridgerton*, many of the debutantes declare their versatile talents to budding suitors. However, it's likely that such self-congratulatory comments would have been perceived as unladylike. The same went for any extreme displays of emotion or spontaneous outbursts. It's no wonder that Daphne's guffaw at the Prince's expense in the ballroom arouses the Queen's disapproval – a woman was always expected to be discreet and reticent in polite society. However, although most of the young debutantes would rather die than do something that attracted attention to themselves, there was one exception: it was perfectly acceptable for a woman to faint or swoon in front of polite society – in fact, it was all but encouraged as it suggested their sensibilities were exceptionally delicate. At the Royal Art exhibit, Cressida Cowper is so overwhelmed by the Prince's romantic overtures, she can but only swoon into his arms gracefully, fortunately with barely a petticoat out of place. It's a talent admired and coveted by many of the debutantes there.

Never Leave Home Without a Chaperone

One of the most crucial practices to protect a young unmarried woman's honour was to ensure she was never left alone in the company of a gentleman without a chaperone. This also limited the number of opportunities for debutantes to fall in love with a man from an inappropriate background or class – lest they do anything particularly crazed such as run off to Gretna Green with an actor or footman.

Normally, a debutante would be chaperoned by her mother, but a maid, groom or relative could also fulfil the role. It was also the chaperone's duty to keep an eagle eye out for any suitable matches, while they were promenading in the park or attending a ball. If the latter, they would stay by the lady's side until she was asked to dance. In between dances, she was allowed to walk about the room with her dancing partner or go for refreshments with them.

In the brief moments where the couple were actually able to have a conversation, there was also a strict code of conduct to follow that sought to quash any romantic desire. Touching was only permitted if the gentleman was being chivalrous – it was acceptable for a man to drape a shawl over a lady's shoulders or assist her when climbing the stairs, entering a carriage or mounting a horse. It was also permissible to link arms while out walking together, but if a man tried to take a lady's hand, she was required to withdraw it disdainfully, regardless of whether or not she wanted to.

When Simon Basset and Daphne Bridgerton become acquainted, it's not long before he asks her to call him by his Christian name. But this was actually forbidden as it suggested the couple were more intimate than was appropriate.

A lady was permitted to drive her own carriage or ride horseback on her family estate but was never allowed to drive on the open road in town without a groom. Women were expected to feign total ignorance about some of the more salacious activities their male counterparts got up to. This is perhaps why they could never be seen alone traversing St James's Street, London, where many of the gentlemen's clubs were located.

Dress Flawlessly

A lady's dress was required to be as refined, elegant and understated as her behaviour. She was expected to be a follower, rather than a leader of fashion – it wasn't acceptable to take a particular trend to excess either for fear of appearing to court attention or admiration.

Ladies were advised to wear clothing that was flattering for their age and colouring and to keep to colours and shades that suited her best. White was believed to be the most flattering colour for young women. However, if they wanted to wear colours, etiquette manuals suggested women with a slight build wear paler shades of green, yellow, lilac and pink, while those with a fuller figure were advised to choose bold crimsons, scarlets and deeper shades of purple and yellow. Large patterns or heavy trimmings were best avoided if you were of small stature.

Alfred E. Douglas, the writer of *The Etiquette of Fashionable Life: Including The Ball Room, and The Court Etiquette of the Present Day*, would have looked on aghast at the Featheringtons' wardrobe as the manual warned women against including clashing or glaring colours in their wardrobe. A lack of judgement in this area was considered to be in bad taste and reeked of snobbery or pretentiousness – attributes no lady wished to be associated with, as they suggested she wasn't secure enough in her status or position.

A lady was also expected to dress in outfits that were appropriate for the time of day and the occasion at hand. If she set off on a country walk in attire that was only suitable for a carriage journey, for example, she would certainly raise a few eyebrows. Likewise, to dress in anything too gaudy during the day when receiving visitors was considered a faux pas.

Ladies were also expected to match their jewellery appropriately with their outfit – *Mixing in Society: A*

Complete Manual of Manners advised that daytime jewellery should be kept to a brooch, watch or bracelet, while anything shiny or expensive should be reserved for the evening. The small and discreet diamond that Daphne wears around her neck on a chain during the day reflects her elegant and refined behaviour – she is the ultimate 'Diamond of the First Water'.

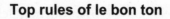

Top rules of le bon ton

- It was considered de rigueur for morning callers to present calling cards with their name, title and residence before they were admitted to a household. The cards were handed to servants but were often displayed on special trays in the front hallway in a sure-fire way to subtly impress other visitors if someone of a particularly high status had paid a call.

- A morning call was not expected to go past half an hour. Certain topics – particularly scandal or gossip – were deemed improper and compliments, however flattering, were to be avoided.

- If a gentleman called on a family, they'd ask for the mistress of the house if it was a social visit, but the master of the house if it was a business call.

- The master of the house received callers in his business room or library, while the mistress received callers in the drawing room. It was completely acceptable for women to carry on with their needlework during a call.

* In London, a lady couldn't pay a call to someone of a higher social standing unless they had called or left a card requiring her presence.

* It wasn't deemed appropriate for a lady, whether single or married, to call at a man's residence.

* Hyde Park was the place to see and be seen. Regency ladies and gentlemen went there on horseback to take in the fresh air (side saddle only of course if you were a lady), show off their clothing in open carriages or promenade for suitors. The fashionable time to visit was between four thirty and seven thirty in the day, though most ladies preferred to make their entrance from about half five onwards.

* Dinner guests were seated in order of rank, with the highest-ranking lady sitting to the right of the host, who always sat at the head. It was considered impolite to talk across the table so conversation was restricted to guests sitting on your left and right.

* Ladies were expected to retire to the drawing room after dinner, leaving men to their port and conversation.

- Debutantes weren't allowed to take part in more than two consecutive dances with the same partner.
- The waltz was considered to be a particularly risqué and intimate dance. Ladies were only allowed to dance with a partner they already knew or had been introduced to.

Chapter 4
Scandals Galore

Today, many celebrities dread the prospect of their private affairs being splashed across the front pages of the tabloid newspapers and it was no different for the haut ton – the celebrities of the day – back in the early 19th century.

If they were lucky, their secrets were whispered behind a fan on the dancefloor or over a hand of cards at a gentlemen's club. But more often than not, their scandalous behaviour was exposed by caricaturists – who were the paparazzi of the day – such as Thomas Rowlandson, George Cruikshank and James Gillray. Their skewered depictions of politicians, socialites and members of the royal family were splayed all over the windows of London's print shops. Here, they attracted huge crowds of intrigued onlookers, who delighted in finding out about the latest exploits of high society.

The audience and appetite for these images was huge. Advances in the printing press made it possible and more affordable for people to buy their own etchings and engravings – a plain print typically cost sixpence, while a coloured one was a shilling. Gillray's 'The Jersey Smuggler Detected' was particularly popular and depicted the Prince Regent caught in bed with his mistress, Lady Jersey, by his wife, Caroline.

As the commercial press expanded during the late 18th century, it became clear that the love lives and associated scandals of high society figures were guaranteed to boost sales. Although the Regency era didn't have whole newspapers dedicated to gossip like today, many featured news and columns about the lives of the wealthy and aristocratic. One of the earliest examples of tabloid journalism was *Town & Country Magazine*'s much-loved 'Histories of the Tête-à-Tête' column, which exposed the salacious goings-on of a different couple each month. It was launched after Lord Grosvenor, who owned most of Mayfair, was discovered to be a regular visitor to backstreet brothels.

Le bon ton anticipated the column as hotly as Lady Whistledown's scandal sheets. From infidelities to bankruptcy, elopements and disreputable acts, they relished gossip as much as the next person – just so long as they weren't on the receiving end of it, of course. Although people weren't named outright, to avoid libel laws, their identities were often thinly veiled through nicknames or unflattering descriptions. In fact, half the fun for readers was figuring out who the papers were referring to. So, who were the royals and aristocrats who shocked and delighted Georgian Britain with their scandalous stories?

George, Prince of Wales (King George IV)

The Prince Regent was the eldest son of King George III and Queen Charlotte. When his father was deemed too mentally unstable to rule, he was sworn in as Regent, aged 48, in 1811. But the Prince proved to be an ineffective monarch whose self-indulgence and extravagance made him incredibly unpopular with his subjects. Stories of his excesses in food and drink, as well as his numerous affairs, were rarely out of the gossip columns. His opulent lifestyle and ever-expanding waistline earned him many unflattering nicknames, which included the 'Prince of Whales'.

In 1795, due to mounting debts, George was forced to marry Princess Caroline of Brunswick. It was to prove a disastrous and loveless union and the Prince went on to have a string of mistresses. These included his mother's friend Lady Jersey (Frances Villiers) and his former lover Maria Fitzherbert, whom he married illegally in 1785. When he had an affair with the actress Mary Robinson, the couple were referred to as 'Perdita' – after one of her most well-known roles – and 'Florizel', which was one of the pet names she gave him.

The Prince, however, did have some redeeming qualities. He was a huge supporter of art, architecture, music and science, and invested vast sums in creating many of the culturally significant sites we enjoy today. His legacies include the Brighton Pavilion, Regent's Park (named after him) and the National Portrait Gallery.

Prince Frederick, Duke of York and Albany, and Mary Anne Clarke

Criminal conversation (a euphemism for adultery) was a common occurrence among le bon ton and perhaps unsurprisingly, their attitude towards it was fairly hypocritical. As long as members of the ton kept up appearances on the surface, what they got up to behind closed doors was generally overlooked, especially if they were of noble birth. But there were even some members of the royal family who couldn't be cushioned from the fallout of scandal. In 1809, the Duke of York – the Regent's brother and commander-in-chief of the British Army – found himself at the centre of a huge monetary scandal involving his mistress, Mary Anne Clarke.

Clarke's origins were humble – the daughter of a London stonemason, she became an established actress and a regular on the courtesan scene before attracting the Duke's attentions. As was common practice for members of the royal family and aristocracy, he installed his mistress in a private residence and set her up with a monthly allowance. However, it proved insufficient to support her expensive tastes. As the coffers began to dwindle, she took up a hustle to earn extra, selling military commissions and promotions on the side. When the affair ended unceremoniously, she let slip what she'd been up to and a public inquiry ensued. After a series of Frederick's love letters to her were printed in the gossip columns, he was forced to resign from his military post.

Frederick, Lord Viscount Bolingbroke, and Lady Diana Spencer

Viscount Bolingbroke, dubbed 'Bully the Battersea Baron', was known primarily for the racehorses he bred and his string of mistresses. He saw no reason to drop the latter after his marriage to Lady Diana Spencer in 1757, nor indeed his addiction to gambling. After he infected his wife with venereal disease, she began a long and passionate affair with Topham Beauclerk, a celebrated wit of the day. The Viscount sued his wife's lover, with whom she bore a child, for 'criminal conversation' and evidence of their clandestine encounters was trawled through court by servant testimonies – details included dirty marks on a parlour coach and scattered cushions all over the floor. In 1768, the couple divorced.

Hugh Percy, 2nd Duke of Northumberland, and Lady Anne Crichton-Stuart

British Army officer and peer Hugh Percy was the son of the Duke of Northumberland and one of the wealthiest men in England. In 1779, he filed for divorce after his wife, Lady Anne, was discovered in bed with a Cambridge University student. Aside from his wealth, Percy was also known for his temper.

One wonders just how incensed he was when *Town & Country Magazine* alleged he was impotent due to excessive masturbation as a schoolboy.

The Marquis of Blandford and Mary Ann Sturt

The Marquis of Blandford found himself at the mercy of many a cheese-related joke when it emerged that he'd seduced Lady Mary Ann Sturt with love letters hidden in gifts of Parmesan. He was so in love with her that he vowed to give up his inheritance if she eloped with him – he was heir to a dukedom and Blenheim Palace. However, Mary's MP husband, Charles Sturt, took legal action and Blandford was ordered to pay £100 in damages for his infidelity. Like many others of his aristocratic contemporaries he racked up huge debts, which left him impoverished. The couple never eloped or married but had six children together and lived out their final years in relative happiness at Blenheim Palace.

Augustus Henry FitzRoy, 3rd Duke of Grafton

The British prime minister, the 3rd Duke of Grafton, was one figure who paid little heed to le bon ton's golden rule of discretion. In 1769, he divorced his wife, Anne, after she gave birth to the Earl of Upper Ossory's child. However, Grafton was not beyond reproach himself. He'd been carrying on a very public five-year affair with a courtesan, Nancy Parsons. Despite his position and standing, they appeared openly together in high society and hosted lavish parties.

The papers decried Grafton's hedonistic behaviour and public opinion turned against him. With his attention so obviously distracted from running the country, he was deemed unfit to govern. But it was his flouting of society's unspoken rule that seemed to attract the most acerbic criticism. As the anonymous writer Junius commented in the *Public Advertiser*: 'There is a certain outrage to decency which for the benefit of society should never be forgiven. It is not that he kept a mistress at home, but that he constantly attended her abroad. It is not the private indulgence, but the public insult, of which I complain.'

Lady Caroline Lamb and Lord Byron

Emotional outbursts, or 'histrionic' behaviour, in public were also judged extremely harshly by society. Lady Caroline Lamb was an intelligent, beautiful and vivacious woman, whose verbal wit and charms attracted the celebrated poet of the day, Lord Byron. When they met in 1812, she was already married to William Lamb and Byron was a literary sensation whose publication of *Childe Harold's Pilgrimage, Cantos I & II* had earned him overnight success.

Everybody wanted a piece of Byron and Lady Caroline famously dubbed him 'mad, bad, and dangerous to know'. The couple soon began a romantic, yet ultimately destructive liaison. After five months, Byron broke off their relationship and began to pursue Annabella Milbanke, who would eventually become his wife. Lamb was distraught and broke down. Psychiatrists at the time called her illness 'erotomania' – a rare type of dementia caused by an obsession for a man.

The gossip sheets relished the melodrama surrounding the demise of the couple's passionate affair. In the aftermath they were relatively sympathetic towards the heartbroken Lamb or 'Caro', as she now called herself – it had been Byron's pet name for her. Lamb's husband, William, took her to Ireland to recover and take her out of the public spotlight. However, she and Byron continued to write to each other.

When Caroline returned to London, Byron made it clear their relationship was over for good, but she refused to accept it. Any public or tabloid sympathy for her soon turned to disgust after she made a series of public attempts to reunite with him. Matters came to a head in 1813 at a ball. After Byron publicly insulted her, Lamb tried to slash her wrists with a broken wine glass. Polite society was scandalised by the incident and what they perceived to be the spurned lover's attention-grabbing behaviour. As Byron himself remarked, 'Lady Caroline performed the dagger scene' – a nod to the famous scene in Shakespeare's *Macbeth*.

In 1816, Lamb sealed her fate when she published the romantic novel *Glenarvon*. The book is full of characters based on figures from her own life and high society. Many of them were easily recognisable and viciously satirised by her. It was an instant success but she would remain a social outcast for the rest of her life.

Harriette Wilson

The famed Regency courtesan Harriette Wilson took public shaming a step further than Lady Caroline Lamb when she published her kiss'n'tell memoirs in 1825. It named many of the distinguished figures she'd had relationships with and included frank and witty details regarding their intimate encounters.

The daughter of a shopkeeper, Wilson was an adventurous, intelligent and unconventional woman who decided she wouldn't settle for life as a governess or any of the options society afforded a woman of her birth. At the age of 15, she became William, Lord Craven's mistress and firmly established herself in high society as one of the most sought-after courtesans of the Regency era. Harriette enjoyed a lavish lifestyle and was promised future security by her many prospective suitors, with whom she set up proper financial contracts. However, by the time she turned 40, she was on the edge of poverty and the men who had promised to look after her had reneged on their commitments. Wilson set to work writing her memoirs, not before contacting her former lovers to let them know she'd gladly spare them, if they paid her £200.

One of her old regulars just so happened to be Arthur Wellesley, 1st Duke of Wellington, who had gone on to become the nation's hero and was now a member of the Tory Cabinet. He refused to be blackmailed and responded in short shrift with 'publish and be damned', which he scrawled on the back of an envelope. Wilson went on to follow his order and didn't spare him in her candid descriptions. She compared his pillow talk to 'like sitting up with a corpse' and said he reminded her of a 'rat catcher' when they first met. Perhaps unsurprisingly, invites to polite society dos for Harriette soon dried up after that, her memoirs became a bestseller and she enjoyed immense wealth for the rest of her life.

As much as people enjoyed reading scandalous stories about the elite, wealthy and powerful, public opinion was beginning to turn against them. Each story was further proof that they weren't the deified figures they claimed to be. In 1830, riots broke out across England when the House of Lords rejected voting reforms. Two years later, the Great Reform Act of 1832 was passed. It introduced major changes to the electoral system of England and Wales and marked an important step towards reducing the amount of power held by the aristocracy.

Mixed Messages:
A Quiz for Modern Flirters

In the days before social media or mobile phones, men and women whispered their indiscretions and greatest secrets behind fluttering fans, or in the boxes of the opera house. But just imagine if such technology had existed in the days of *Bridgerton* – they wouldn't have had to wait for a horse-drawn Royal Mail coach to deliver their important message. What innermost thoughts and desires do you think they'd communicate? See if you can match the correct character to the correct message:

(a) 'Darling, your rendition of *Quante Volte* tonight was so earth-shattering, I think Vesuvius has just erupted again! Meet me later and let us shelter from the destruction of the fallout in your dressing room.'

(b) 'We need to talk. I cannot promise a table or two won't get smashed to smithereens in the process. Meet me in White's at 9, you rake – if you dare!'

(c) 'Colin, I'm hiding in the outhouse – any chance you could sneak me out a beer? I don't think I can bear being introduced to yet another insipid daughter of an Earl!'

(d) 'I must confess, I'm not sure this is what normally happens when one looks at a piece of artwork but I definitely felt a strange quivering within me I'd not experienced before. Perhaps I should limit my visits to Somerset House, as it was most peculiar. Has this ever happened to you? And no, before you ask, I'm sure it had nothing to do with the company I was in attendance with.'

(e) 'I must say, his dance moves are wonderfully adept but husband material? Don't be ridiculous! I don't believe there is ever such a thing as a reformed rake.'

(f) 'Yes, the grounds of his home are wonderful, with plenty of space to wander in and breathe in the fresh air. And his outdoor gazebo proved most practical when we managed to shelter there one evening, after an unexpected shower caught us off guard.'

(g) 'The act! The act! One hears a lot of the marriage act, but what actually is the act?! I wish someone would elucidate me on this matter. But when I try to ask Mama she just goes a bit red and starts blabbering on about some farm we visited when I was a child. Have you any idea what a farm's got to do with it? Does one purchase farmyard animals when one gets married? I do not understand!'

(h) 'So, the act has happened. All I can say is, I know now why Mama found it so difficult to put into words. I'm not sure there are words sufficient enough. ☺ Now, I understand.'

(i) 'I must confess she is rather pleasing to the eye and is able to sustain my attention for longer periods than your average chit can, with her amusing observations. But as we know, the question at the forefront of any young lady's mind is: "Is he good enough to marry and will he sire an heir?" I, of course, am adamant I'll do neither.'

(j) 'I have to confess, the way she straddled that horse so expertly when she swept into the middle of that ridiculous duel did get my mind racing. I clear forgot what a little idiot she was for getting involved. With my senses so befuddled, I can think that's the only goddamn reason I agreed to marry her.'

(k) 'If only her mother would stop insisting she wears that rather putrid yellow, she might have a little more chance attracting suitors. It's most frightfully unbecoming for her skin tone. Still, I suppose it's one less competitor in the running for the Prince's affections!'

(l) 'What I wouldn't have given for a winged demon to push her down those goddamn stairs when she came gliding down them so perfectly! She stole the Prince right from under my perfectly powdered nose! I'm so angry, I'd like to shove her feathered headdress where daylight can never reacheth!'

(m) 'My heart beats so ardently for him but he barely notices me. I'm just his sister's little friend. One day I hope he'll admire me as much as a Michelangelo statue or a Botticelli painting he'll see on his travels. Until then, I'll have to settle for getting his attention by other means.'

(n) 'When I write, I feel truly able to express myself. A different persona emerges – I feel powerful, of high status, with a sense of belonging. I'm no longer just the ugly duckling or "the clever one", (not difficult in my family, admittedly). The pen is my weapon against society.'

(o) 'If this is what every ball is going to be like then I may as well spend my evening in the company of parading peacocks in Richmond Park. With all this squawking, I fear my eardrums might burst by sundown. I'm currently seeking refuge at the lemonade table for fear I might suffocate on one of the many feathers in this room, or get my toes trampled on in the stampede to find an eligible suitor. I'd love to pop out for a cheeky cigarette but I fear Mama will spot me. She's keeping an eagle eye on me at present.'

(p) 'I asked him if he'd read *Candide* by Voltaire and he replied that he definitely doesn't have a fungal disease. What's the point of educating one's self if you can't even converse decently with any of these buffoons?!'

(q) 'It's quite obvious he's in love with her, the fool, but no doubt he'll go gallivanting off again around Europe to "find himself". When he's already found what he's truly looking for. Love. And it's standing right in front of him.'

(r) 'Mrs Featherington would do well to rein in her extravagant wardrobe as tightly as she reins her daughters into their corsets. I hear her husband was gambling in White's at the weekend yet again.'

(s) 'Tell me, my dear, I spied you taking tea earlier in Gunter's. What exactly was on that silver spoon that caused you to lick it for so long and so lasciviously? Have you recently acquired an appetite for the taste of precious metals, since returning from your recent trip visiting the antiquities? Or did you simply wish to give a certain young lady something to think on if she's struggling to sleep at night?'

(t) 'No matter their aptitude for the pianoforte, embroidery or watercolour painting, I can't sustain his attention in any of them for longer than two seconds. Still, my list continues to grow. Ultimately, of course, I'd prefer that he marries for love but he needs to take responsibility and settle down at some point.'

(u) 'She needs to get the ridiculous notion of marrying for love out of that ignorant head of hers. There are far worse fates in life than waking up each morning to the craggy and weathered face of an old man. Namely ending up in the slums and ending up a Haymarket ware!'

(v) 'He's completely ruined us! That gambling, useless bilk has made a complete mull of it all. No matter how sweetly my dear daughters sing at the pianoforte, they'll never find suitable matches now!'

(w) 'Ooh la la! My big faradiddle [lie] has been rumbled. If Lady Whistledown finds out about this, I'm done for. Once they know I'm just an ordinary English commoner, I'll lose all my business!'

(x) 'Well, I must say, I'm still in high ropes after my oil painting class last night. I knew life models were renowned for being a little louche and libertine but I certainly learnt a lot more about female anatomy than I was bargaining for at the after party.'

(y) 'I'm having the most amusing time sitting on the sofa watching a string of suitors visit Daphne to declare their undying love and devotion. God, I pray that I never fall so hard for someone that I become deluded enough to believe I can write a sonnet to rival Shakespeare!'

(z) 'What news, my love, from the battlefield? The thought of you and our days sharing cake together in church are the only memories that keep me sane at night.'

Take a break and colour in these wallpaper-worthy patterns.

Take a break and colour in these wallpaper-worthy patterns.

Chapter 5
Fan Flirting, Reticules and Handkerchiefs

How to Win Fans with the Fan

There were certain accessories no genteel lady of the 'ton', the upper echelon of English society, would ever dare leave her home without. Whether promenading the banks of the Thames for potential suitors, or taking a turn around the ballroom (with one eye discreetly surveying the talent), the fan was one of the most indispensable items in a lady's reticule (that's 'Regency handbag' to you and me). It could provide immediate relief from the rays of the sun, the stifling heat of an overcrowded ballroom or the burning gaze radiating from an eligible bachelor across the dancefloor.

But in the days before telecommunications, it was also an extremely handy tool (no pun intended) for signalling interest or indifference to members of the opposite sex. Regency ladies were expected to be chaste and quiet, so any overtly flirtatious behaviour on their part would be frowned upon in their social circles. But fan-flirting was a subtle and accepted way for a lady to elicit attention, relay messages and ward off the competition – as well as an excellent opportunity to show off her impeccably manicured nails and delicate, soft hands.

Regency ladies practised the art of fan control at great length in front of a mirror before they unleashed their skills in secret conversation onto society – some moves were even said to take three months to master! Whether the men were equally well-versed in fan etiquette is another matter. But for any lady who hadn't yet mastered the art of fan-flirting, it was best she left her fan furled or slipped over her wrist – lest any aimless movements resulted in confusion or ruffled feathers.

So, should one twirl, furl, open or close?

The secret language of fan flirting

Unscramble these two lists to match the gesture to what it means:

Gesture	Meaning
Hold fan in front of the face with the left hand	Please be aware that my chaperone is keeping a watchful eye on me.
Hold fan near to left ear	I'd like to get to know you better, come and talk to me.
Twirl fan in right hand	You seem a little too eager for my liking.
Gaze at closed fan	I'm terribly sorry but my heart belongs to another.
Carry fan in right hand	You seem to have misunderstood me.
Twirl fan in the left hand	I'd really rather you placed your attentions elsewhere.
Drop the fan	I'm off to the lemonade table for some refreshment, please follow my lead.

Hold fan in front of the face with the right hand	You are nothing but a rake and I know it.
Close the fan extremely slowly	I am betrothed to someone else.
Let the fan rest on left cheek	Yes.
Let the fan rest on right cheek	No.
Fan slowly	I betroth myself to you and promise to be your wife.
Fan quickly	I am already married.
Place fan behind head	You have permission to kiss me.
Place handle of fan to the lips	My heart is in your hands.
Draw fan across the cheek	Your behaviour towards me is somewhat vulgar.
Draw fan through the hand	What are your true feelings towards me?
Present shut	We will be friends.

Open and shut	I'm currently occupied with an utter bore but please don't take your leave just yet.
Draw fan across the eyes	You are permitted to come and talk to me.
Hold fan wide open	Please forgive my dalliance.
Touch fan with the tip of finger	I think you're most becoming and you've caught my eye, please request an introduction.

Of course, not just any old fan would do. The look and feel of a fan were as important as what you did with it. The 19th-century 'Vernis Martin' style of fan was particularly coveted for its innovative varnishing technique, which allowed vibrant colours to be preserved on a variety of materials – ivory, tortoiseshell, mother of pearl, even chicken skin. Delicate and discreet works of art, they were often hand painted with Oriental scenes. Some of them featured paintings by the celebrated neo-classical artist Angela Kauffmann RA (1741–1807).

Fans could also be fringed with feathers – not dissimilar to the one that Daphne weaponises in her quest to find love again, after Simon cruelly rejects her. As she glides down the staircase in her glittery white ballgown, no one can take their eyes off her – least of all, Prince Frederick of Prussia. Despite his superior standing, he is powerless in her presence. Daphne's victory is sealed the moment she drops her fan at his feet and he stoops instantly to retrieve it – a flawless demonstration in the art of fan control.

Reticules at Dawn: The Regency Handbag

Reticules were drawstring purses made of lace and velvet, resembling a type of pocket that would traditionally have been worn as an undergarment. They were originally designed to complement the trend in women's fashion towards plainer and more lightweight muslin dresses – underskirt pockets didn't suit a flatter silhouette, so these were created as an alternative.

Ladies liked to brand or personalise their reticules with their own embroidered or beaded decorations and designs. Initially, they were seen as quite a shocking accompaniment to a woman's attire, as the habit of carrying items in pockets and bags was viewed as a typically masculine one. But as the reticule grew in popularity, it soon became known as the 'indispensable', a necessary, as well as aesthetically pleasing, addition to any lady's wardrobe. It was also often referred to as the 'ridicule'; the reasons for this remain unclear although historians have suggested it's because their small size meant they were often overstuffed with items – not a dissimilar problem to the one some people face today with their handbags!

Smelling salts (snuff), coins and handkerchiefs were just a few of the indispensable items you might find in a lady's Regency handbag.

Hanky Panky

Today, it seems peculiar to find anything romantic about handkerchiefs – indeed, many would describe them as nothing more than a 'glorified germ carrier'. But throughout the Georgian period it was customary for ladies to embroider them with symbols of romance or messages of love before gifting to a loved one. Some went even further and created handkerchiefs out of locks of their own hair. But just like the fan, ladies of the ton could also employ this simple little piece of cotton fabric to signal feelings of affection, devotion or even revulsion towards the opposite sex.

The secret language of handkerchief flirting

Unscramble these two lists to match the gesture to what it means:

Gesture	Meaning
Draw across the cheek	I'm engaged.
Put in the pocket	I'm married.
Fold	You have my cheek.
Draw across the eyes	You disgust me!
Draw across the forehead	I'm sorry, please forgive me.
Draw through the hands	I'd like to be introduced to you.
Draw across the lips	I'd like to speak with you.
Twist in the right hand	I've no love to offer you at this time.
Wind around the forefinger	My chaperone is near.
Wind around the third finger	My heart belongs to another.

Take the Test:
In Want of a Wife?

It is a truth rather begrudgingly acknowledged – in regency fiction, at least – that a reformed rake in possession of a questionable sexual past will make a damn fine husband. It takes a proper diamond like Daphne, of course, to make Simon renounce his penchant for romping all over the ruins of Europe – he won't just give up his bad-boy ways for anyone. Luckily for Daphne, she gets to benefit from all those years of experience sowing his wild oats.

Should a lady ever take the risk of ruin though? Can a rake ever really redeem himself? Or is he – as Eliza Bisbee Duffey warned in *What Women Should Know: A Woman's Book About Women* – just taking a temporary break to curb his physical exhaustion? Before you say yes to a proposal from the neighbourhood bad boy, take this quiz. Is he really in want of a wife and ready to settle down, or does he just want a moment's peace from his ambitious mama?

1. You're flicking through some brochures for holiday inspiration. Your rake . . .

   a) Takes you in his arms and locks your eyes with an intense, steely gaze. He says: 'Before I die, I simply must make love to you on the sand dunes of Santorini at sunset. Let's take this chance.'

   b) Turns to you and says: 'Ibiza's always a good laff this time of year. Plus, 24-hour partying so we can get shit-faced the entire time. We can rent my mate's airbnb.'

   c) Becomes completely distracted by his best mate messaging him with images of Riga's red-light district. He finally turns to you and says: 'Tarquin's stag do's gonna be tops!'

2. You're at a friend's wedding. Your rake . . .

   a) Turns to you with tears in his eyes and says: 'I can't wait till the first dance at our wedding. Let's make a list now of our Top Ten favourite songs.'

   b) Remarks on the excellence of the hollandaise sauce and says: 'We should get the caterer's details. You know, just in case.'

   c) Can't stop making louche comments about how hot the groom's mother is, 'for her age'.

3. You get caught in a rainstorm en route to a restaurant. Your rake . . .

   a) Wraps his fur pelisse around your shoulders and orders an Uber to pick up a change of clothes from your home. Spends half the evening drying you with his portable hairdryer.

   b) Suggests you sit in the pub garden next to an outdoor heater.

   c) Leaves you standing on the pavement while he goes to pick up an umbrella from his ex-girlfriend's place round the corner.

4. You're at home in bed, feeling unwell. Your rake . . .

   a) Pops over with a hot water bottle and cooks you a hearty, warming soup. Even though you've got a temperature and a Kleenex shoved halfway up your nose, he perches on the edge of your bed and tells you how beautiful you look.

   b) Pops over, orders you a takeaway and uses the opportunity to catch up on all the episodes of *Top Gear* he's missed.

   c) Doesn't want to risk catching what you've got so he pops out for a night down at White's with his dandy chums.

5. You invite your rake over for a meal with your family. He . . .

   a) Listens attentively to your father as he describes at great length how the regenerative braking in his new BMW works, praises your mum's gooseberry pie and enthrals your little brothers and sisters with his origami ponies. Brings a bottle of vintage Veuve Clicquot.

   b) Arrives with a shop-bought cheesecake and nods politely at everything your parents say.

Feigns interest in your dad's eighties acid house collection.

c) Drinks too much of the champagne he brings and is drunk from 9pm onwards. Argues with your father over the finer points of Wellington's square formation tactics during the Battle of Waterloo. Spends the rest of the evening ogling the pretty servants before smashing your family's 150-year-old whisky decanter.

Mostly As

It's time to celebrate, crack open the Moët and get working on the wedding invite list together. Since finding true love with the girl of his dreams, who he can also happily call his best mate, your former rake has deleted his Tinder account and put his days of womanising far behind him. Clearly, he only has eyes for you. Careful he doesn't go up in flames next time he's in your company!

Mostly Bs

Only time will tell with this one. He's not entirely indifferent but probably not about to set your corset on fire any time soon. There is of course the possibility you're too dazzling a diamond for him to contemplate right now, but perhaps keep an eye out for some more deserving and ardent admirers waiting in the wings of Almack's.

Mostly Cs

Oh dear! Your rake's about as reformed as Casanova on an episode of *Love Island*. His outrageous behaviour raises many an astonished eyebrow wherever he goes, his feelings for you are about as deep and meaningful as his pocket snuff box. Do not mistake his flattery or momentarily intense glances for true love. Your friends and family's concerns are valid. Ignore them at your peril, for they probably know him far better than you think – some in ways you'd probably rather not know about! So, refuse that proposal and get practising your fan flirting again.

Chapter 6
Love and Courtship

After dancing with a selection of eligible suitors, in Season 1, Episode 3 of *Bridgerton*, 'The Art of the Swoon', Daphne remarks wryly to Simon that she thinks she's felt more thrills having her corset tightened at The Modiste.

So, how does she know this? What's missing during these encounters and why do they feel so different to the physical sensations she experiences around the Duke? As Daphne discovers, she has little or no control over what her body experiences every time she's in close proximity to Simon, but she's never felt anything like this before and no one else leaves her feeling so strange. The blushing, flushed skin and raised heartbeat betray her true sensibilities, no matter how hard she tries to conceal them. But are these physical sensations a sure enough sign that she's found the true love she's searching for? As a young and nubile woman of the Regency period, yes!

This was the era that popularised the belief that blushing, swooning, crying and fainting were all symptoms of romantic love. It was also the era that celebrated romantic love as the foundation for a long and happy and successful marriage. Daphne embraces these ideals and she aspires to marry for love, just as her mother did before her. But this concept was still relatively fresh and radical.

During the 17th century in England, marriage was not a romantic endeavour. The upper classes often married within their family to strengthen alliances that would help to secure, or advance, their power, wealth and position. Whether you were in love or not was of little consequence. Suitable matches were often arranged by parents when the couples were still children. However, in the 18th and 19th centuries, people began to embrace the idea of romantic courtship and marrying for love. Indeed, the English novelist Jane Austen, herself a clergyman's daughter, didn't have enough land or dowry to attract a man of noble birth, but she turned down a number of tempting offers from wealthy, well-born men because she couldn't bear 'the misery of being bound without love'.

This change in attitudes was influenced by a movement within art, literature and music that would become known as Romanticism. It grew out of the philosophical works of the French philosopher Jean-Jacques Rousseau (1712–78), who many consider to be the father of the movement. In 1762 he wrote the seminal opening line in his work, *The Social Contract*: 'Man is born free, and he is everywhere in chains.' His ideas challenged the conventions and rules of the establishment and stressed the importance of individual freedom and liberty. The English Romantic poets such as Lord Byron, William Blake, William Wordsworth and John Keats were profoundly inspired by his ideals and propelled the Romantic movement forward.

The Romantics revered nature and the natural world, while renouncing the factories and mills of the industrialised cities with their collectivised workforces. They believed individuals should have the freedom to express their authentic self. Great emphasis was placed on the rich spectrum of emotions that nature and romance could inspire – from joy and excitement to sorrow, anxiety and heartbreak.

In the throes of his love affair with Marina Thompson, Colin Bridgerton declares his heart doesn't listen to his head and when he ends up feeling foolish with a broken heart, Penelope comforts him, telling him that he must never apologise for falling in love. Lady Whistledown refers to the fragility of the human heart throughout the series and the wounding nature of love. But the Romantics were deeply hopeful about marriage and believed that life-long love was possible. Daphne's mother, Lady Violet, advises her to put love at the heart of her marriage – if she chooses to love every day, all their problems will be resolved.

The rise of printing and print culture also contributed to positive representations of marriage. Prints entitled 'Happiness' depicted images of domestic bliss, with married couples in their homes, surrounded by children. The custom to send cards to a loved one on Valentine's Day grew in popularity. Many of the designs featured the same romantic symbols and iconography we recognise today, from Cupid's bow to hearts and flowers, but they also presented images that were popular with the Romantics – lovers sitting underneath trees in a pastoral utopia, surrounded by birds and nature.

Europeans also perceived love to be a measure of how civilised a nation was. Countries that placed love at the heart of marriage were considered to be civilised and virtuous. In contrast, those that practised arranged marriages, or were indifferent to love as a fundamental concept for marriage, were judged as savage or barbarous. Somewhat inevitably, however, issues of social class, religion and background continued to play a huge role in dictating who the upper classes could marry. Romantic love was an ideal to strive for, but it was extremely unlikely that a duchess would ever declare her undying love for a butler or gamekeeper and elope to Gretna Green. Social disparities were reserved for affairs, not courtship. In Jane Austen's classic novel, *Pride and Prejudice*, Charlotte Lucas advises Jane Bennet to secure a rich husband first and concern herself with love only after they are married.

In *The Female Instructor; Or Young Woman's Companion: Being a Guide to All the Accomplishments which Adorn the Female Character* . . ., the author tells women to remain vigilant before they allow their affections to be engaged by a young man: 'Endeavour, in the most prudent and secret manner to procure from your friends every necessary piece of information concerning him; such as his character, as to sense, his morality, his religion, his temper and family; whether it is distinguished for parts and worth, or for folly and knavery.' Women were warned to 'avoid a companion that may entail any hereditary disease on your posterity' (particularly madness) and to steer clear of rakes at all costs: 'He always makes a suspicious husband because he has only known the most worthless of your sex'. Heathens were also off the list: 'If you have a sense of religion yourself, do not think of a husband who has none. If you marry an infidel, or an irreligious character, what hope can you entertain of happiness?'

It was also considered important that family and friends were on board with the marriage too as this was regarded to be the mark of a good match. This was especially important for women as a father could still withhold a fortune from a daughter, although he had no power to disinherit his son from the estate.

This disparity between the sexes continued in other financial matters that influenced the choice of love match. For example, the son of a noble family might be put under pressure to court a merchant's daughter if her fortune was large enough to boost the family's wealth. In contrast, a nobleman's daughter wasn't allowed to marry a merchant – the family wouldn't want their estate or fortune falling into the hands of a 'dealer in trade' as the family name could be affected. Business owners, however wealthy, were deemed to be new money. In *Pride and Prejudice*, Mr Bingley is an example of the nouveau riche, while Mr Darcy is an established and important member of the upper class.

The Stages of Courtship

As we see in *Bridgerton*, a courting couple were subject to endless public scrutiny, but how did an average courtship unfold and what opportunities, if any, were there to build genuine romantic intimacy? Here, a wingman was vital. If a gentleman liked the look of a young lady, he would ask his host or hostess to introduce them.

Test the waters with a gift

After a formal introduction the suitor would signal his interest with a gift – normally he would send something as innocent as a ribbon or a bunch of flowers.

He might also pay a call in the afternoon, though it's unlikely he'd ever recite a sonnet, as one of Daphne's suitors does – this would be perceived as far too presumptuous a move at such an early stage!

Closed carriages were a no-go zone

The couple could get to know each other a little better on a walk, although a chaperone would always remain within earshot. A carriage outing was also permissible, so long as the carriage was open. Who knew what might happen otherwise under this enclosure?

Let's dance

A dance with your beau during a society event and ball was a good opportunity to slip in some compliments or whisper sweet nothings. As Jane Austen's heroine Elizabeth Bennet observes in *Pride and Prejudice*, 'to be fond of dancing was a certain step towards falling in love'. However, courting couples couldn't take more than two consecutive dances in an evening with each other, lest the lady was assumed 'fast'. Even if a couple were already engaged, it was considered to be bad ton.

Sealed with a kiss/a way with words

With the rise in literacy and improvements to Royal Mail post, letters became an increasingly popular way for couples to converse. If a gentleman asked a lady to receive his correspondence, the courtship had certainly moved up a notch too – letters were a good sign that an engagement was on the cards.

Not any old scribbled note would do, though – couples were expected to express their feelings as eloquently as Lord Byron to deepen their romantic bond. Fortunately, there was help at end. *The New Lover's Instructor; or Whole Art of Courtship* contained templates of fictional letters to guide people in the art of letter writing during courtship. Many bestsellers of the day, such as Jane Austen's *Pride and Prejudice*, popularised letter writing as an art form too – as well as moving the plot along or conveying information, they were an opportunity for characters to declare their true feelings articulately.

A token of my love

As the romantic bond intensified, the couple would exchange gifts that reflected this. It was customary to send each other locks of hair or portrait miniatures of themselves. They were often worn as a necklace so their loved one was always close to their heart. Sometimes, lovers would keep a lock of hair in them too. Their popularity peaked at around 1830 before they all but disappeared with the advent of photography. Other popular gifts included snuff boxes or gloves that were often decorated with romantic motifs.

Rules of engagement

Once a couple were engaged, they could call each other by their first names, though only when they were out of the public eye. An engagement didn't give them carte blanche to start piling on the PDAs or canoodle behind a candelabra either. Not surprisingly, they were still expected to be discreet and avoid any overt displays of affection.

The Not-so Romantic Stuff

The length of courtship could vary from between one year to four. Once the father of the young woman had consented to the marriage, legal documents were drawn up that detailed the amount of dowry she would bring. Lord Byron famously received a settlement of £20,000 from the parents of Annabella Milbanke, which would be worth about £800,000 today. This was not enough to cover his spiralling debts, however.

Wedding day

Typically, engagements were short and couples often married within a month. St George's Hanover Square was a favourite church for aristocrats to marry. Weddings were not the bonanzas they were today, though. Even the Prince of Wales (before he became regent), who was well-known for his excess, married at St James's Palace in a simple ceremony with just a handful of people present.

The fashion for white wedding dresses didn't come into vogue until the Victorian era. Most Regency brides married in their Sunday best with little more than a bonnet to crown their head. There were exceptions to this though – the infamous noblewoman Lady Caroline Ponsonby wore a dress of white muslin and lace when she married William Lamb in June 1805.

Bestsellers of the Day

Many courting couples drew romantic inspiration from classic literature and popular novels of the day. Even back then, a suitor could see the advantages in emulating the virtues of *Pride and Prejudice*'s hero Mr Darcy. And although the notorious wet shirt scene never appeared in the original novel, there were still plenty of passages deemed worthy of underscoring. So, who were the romantic heroes and heroines that got the hearts of young lovers racing during the Regency era?

Jean-Jacques Rousseau – *Julie; or The New Heloise* (1761)

One of the first runaway bestsellers, it proved so popular that the publishers couldn't print copies fast enough and had to rent the book out by the hour. The novel explores the passionate yet doomed love affair between a tutor and a young aristocrat named Julie. It follows the characters as they navigate the inner struggle between passion and virtue, and the purity of their soul. People in their droves wrote to Rousseau to describe the intensity of feelings and emotions they experienced while reading the novel.

Classic quotes

'Virtue is a state of war, and to live in it means one always has some battle to wage against oneself.'

'O love! If I long for the days when one savors thee, it is not for the hour of ecstasy; it is for the hour that follows it.'

William Shakespeare – *Romeo and Juliet* (between 1591 and 1596)

Probably the most famous love story of all time, this classic tale of two star-crossed lovers contains some of the most beautiful declarations of love ever written. Shakespeare's reworkings of other classic tragedies such as *Troilus and Cressida* were also extremely popular to quote from.

Classic quotes

'See how she leans her cheek upon her hand.

O, that I were a glove upon that hand.

That I might touch that cheek!'
'Love is a smoke made with the fumes of sighs.'

Johann Wolfgang von Goethe – *The Sorrows of Young Werther* (1774)

This tragic tale of unrequited love tells the story of a young man who falls in love with a woman betrothed to another man. Unable to reconcile they can never be together, he takes his own life. Almost overnight, it turned Goethe into a literary celebrity. Men all over Europe succumbed to Werther fever, dressing in the style of the tragic hero and there were reputed incidences of copycat suicide.

Classic quotes

'I have so much in me, and the feeling for her absorbs it all; I have so much, and without her it all comes to nothing.'

'I am proud of my heart alone, it is the sole source of everything, all our strength, happiness and misery.'

'One hundred times have I been on the point of embracing her. Heavens! What a torment it is to see so much loveliness passing and repassing before us, and yet not dare to lay hold of it! And laying hold is the most natural of human instincts. Do not children touch everything they see? And I!'

Jane Austen – *Pride and Prejudice* (1813)
With over 20 million copies sold, Jane Austen's most famous romantic novel of manners continues to be a bestseller today. First published in 1813, the central plot revolves around the attractive and witty Elizabeth Bennet, who is determined to marry for love despite societal and family pressures to do otherwise. One of literature's best-loved heroines, she is admired the world over for her wit and perception.

Classic quotes
'You must allow me to tell you how ardently I admire and love you.'

'Do not consider me now as an elegant female, intending to plague you, but as a rational creature, speaking the truth from her heart.'

'Their eyes instantly met, and the cheeks of both were overspread with the deepest blush.'

A Checklist for True Love

Do you burn brighter than the gas-lit streets of London's Pall Mall for your new love interest, or have you felt more sparks brushing your teeth with an electric toothbrush? Check to see if you've a love match as electrifying as Daphne and Simon's.

Every time you see their name in your inbox or you accidentally meet them on the street, you bust another bone in your corset. Your friends have all nicknamed you 'Swoony Sue' and you have the Emergency Services on speed dial. ☐

They can make topics that previously bored you sound fascinating. Not least the length of standard gauge used in Robert Stephenson's steam locomotive, *The Rocket*. ☐

During needlework class, your mind is wandering more than usual. Your governess raises an extremely concerned eyebrow at just how awry your tulip embroidery has gone. ☐

You can find yourself gazing at sunsets and listening to birdsong with a renewed, childlike sense of awe and wonderment. Oh, if only they were there to experience it with you! ☐

When you manage to calm down long enough to hold a conversation with them, the time flies by. You make each other laugh so much with your witty observations on the trivialities of Regency courtship, you begin to wonder if it's legal to have this much fun. ☐

A good-looking and eligible prince makes his intentions towards you clear. Sure, the weight of a diamond and sapphire necklace around your neck feels pretty good and you wouldn't half mind being a princess, but Mrs . . . just rolls off the tongue so much better. ☐

You find you're getting a lot less sleep than you used to. And you don't think it's got anything to do with too much exposure to blue light from your iPhone. ☐

You're confused. It's normally only your best mate who makes you laugh and smile this much. Yet, you also desperately want to rip their breeches off. What is this new phenomenon, Mama? ☐

Now count up the number of questions you checked off as a 'yes' to work out your current love match:

0 to 3

You're clearly not quite yourself, but you may just need to up your daily dose of vitamins.

3 to 6

There's certainly enough steam in the engine to get *The Rocket* from Manchester to Liverpool – worth pursuing!

6 to 9

It's a wonder you're not at Clyvedon Castle already, living out your wildest dreams – you're off the charts on the checklist for true lurve.

Play the Game: Rakes & Ladders

Will you ruin your reputation indulging in a dalliance with a rake, or climb the social ladder all the way to the top? Find out what fate has in store for you. Roll the dice to start navigating your way around the highs and lows of Regency high society!

21	22
20 Momentarily, you forget all your fan moves and accidentally tell a persistent baron you love him. He comes barrelling over immediately.	**19** A long line of handsome suitors visit your drawing room after they see you dancing with the Duke. You impress them all with your pianoforte.
11	**12**
10	**9** You play pianoforte so well, Queen Charlotte asks you to entertain her at court. Every member of the ton declares you the 'Diamond of the Season'.
1 You're off to the first ball of the season, dressed in a beautiful ball-gown and feathered headdress.	**2**

24	25
Your feathered headdress falls off at court and almost suffocates one of Queen Charlotte's Pomeranians. You're instantly blacklisted for the season.	
17	16
	You drop your handkerchief on the dancefloor with the initials of your secret love upon it. Lady Whistledown announces your affair in her next gossip sheet.
14	15
7	6
the garden, you find yourself dmiring more than the roses – ith a rakish former friend of your rother's. Can pistols at dawn save our honour?	
4	5
	You attract the attention of a handsome duke with some expert fan flirting. He asks you to dance and you enjoy a romantic waltz.

Chapter 7
It's Fashion, Darling

From feathered headpieces to corsets and extravagantly embroidered Empire dresses, viewers across the world were as captivated by *Bridgerton*'s costumes and accessories as they were by the central love story. Since airing, there's been a resurgence of interest in Regency fashions as people seek to play and experiment with the trends of the early 19th century. But how did political and cultural events of the time influence the fashions and styles of the era? Just as the desire for female emancipation shortened the hems of the twenties flapper dresses, there were significant events that left an undeniable mark on the looks we've come to know and love.

The Discovery of Ancient Roman Ruins

The discovery of Pompeii and Herculaneum in the mid 18th century had a profound impact on European culture. Both cities had been destroyed by a volcanic eruption at Mount Vesuvius in 79 AD. As archaeologists excavated the ruins, they discovered works of art and treasures buried beneath that were completely intact and more beautiful than anything they'd discovered before or could have previously imagined. The fascination for classical antiquity wasn't new – it had influenced many of the great works of art and architecture throughout the Renaissance period – but the discoveries sparked a revival of interest in Greco-Roman culture.

People – the majority of whom were wealthy young men – flocked to visit the historic sites and see the buildings, paintings and sculptures for themselves. They began to incorporate extended visits to existing sites that had already been discovered and highly cultural cities across Italy, renowned for their art and historic buildings. Often they would return with souvenirs picked up on their travels and so the Grand Tour was born. But the discoveries resulted in more than just an enjoyable field trip for the elite and wealthy – a neoclassical revolution swept across Western Europe impacting art, architecture, philosophy and literature. The curves and gaudy, decorative frills of the Baroque and Rococo periods were out. Clean, straight, plain lines and geometric motifs were in. The predominant features of Georgian architecture – linear designs, symmetrical columns and colonnades – were inspired by classical buildings but also reflected simplicity, harmony and rationality, all virtues that people associated with the classical period.

The upper classes and growing affluent middle classes sought to emulate these ideals through their behaviour, thinking and everyday dress. Throughout the late 18th century, the panniers and hooped petticoats that enhanced or expanded the width of women's dresses were rejected in favour of clothing that revealed and accentuated the natural figure.

At the beginning of the 19th century, Empire-style dresses became hugely popular. The long, high-waisted gowns featured small, short sleeves and lower necklines, which were designed to reflect the grace and fluidity of classical sculptures. Lawn and batiste fabrics were used, but muslin was the most popular material of choice as it was easy to clean and emulated the flowing, loose drapery of Greek and Roman statues. It was often white to denote high social status. However, these garments were normally restricted to evening attire as women were expected to wear long sleeves and higher necklines during the day to conserve their modesty – arms, neck and bosom were usually only unveiled in the evening. Indeed, their morning dress had to be short enough to walk in, but long enough not to reveal the ankle. The corset was still required to push up the bosom and flatten the stomach to create the silhouette needed for the dresses.

Embroideries on the hems and borders of the dresses were also influenced by simple, classical Greek patterns. Between 1804 and 1807, a trend developed for Egyptian and Etruscan decorations. The patterns were inspired by gifts Napoleon Bonaparte brought back for his Empress wife, Josephine, after he invaded and occupied Egypt in 1798. As the Regency era progressed, dress designs became more elaborate. Accessories such as the flounce – a gathered frill or ruffle – were attached to the sleeves and hems of ladies' dresses. The emphasis on trim and decoration reflected a move away from the neoclassical influence to one that favoured a more Romantic style. Separate skirts and bodices were also introduced and dresses with a much lower waistline became popular.

In the show, the costume designers wanted to create styles that took inspiration from the historical period that a more contemporary audience could also relate to. The classic Empire silhouette was transformed with many modern and flamboyant elements inspired by Christian Dior collections from the fifties and sixties. They rejected muslin in favour of velvets and stiffer, sheer fabrics – organza, organdie and tulle – that gave the dresses more movement and fluidity.

Bonnets were another Regency staple that were done away with in the show. But the designers referenced them with bonnet-shaped hair accessories made of straw and accented with flowers and feathers.

The French Revolution and Napoleonic Wars

The upper classes of English society had a long-held affinity for, and fascination with, French culture, fashion and art. Great emphasis was placed on learning the language and many in high society spoke it with ease. Revered as the masters of romance, elegance and good taste, courting couples routinely dropped phrases or extracts from French poems into their love letters.

A French chef, patissier or confectioner was considered to be a status symbol in aristocratic homes. In the years following the French Revolution, there was no shortage of them as thousands of French émigrés fled the country to escape the Terror – a period of intense violence and conflict, where those regarded as 'Enemies of the Revolution' were executed.

Dressmakers and milliners also emigrated to England, where they set up shop in the most sought-after areas of London and Bath. It's no surprise that *Bridgerton*'s modiste Madame Delacroix invents an elegant French name and persona for herself to attract the crème de la crème of society ladies – French dressmakers were considered to have exceptional taste and talent.

In England, there were mixed reactions to the French Revolution. It was heralded by reformers as the dawn of a new era that signified freedom and the inevitable progress of enlightenment. But not surprisingly, politicians with aristocratic connections feared revolution in their own country and the end of European civilisation. Either way, England's fascination with French culture and fashion saw no signs of diminishing. The revolt against the established order in France and the changes this brought to their style and fashion had a direct impact on English garments too.

Clothing had long been a visible mark of social privilege, but now members of the French aristocracy no longer wanted to be identified. Increasingly, expensive silks, velvets and other costly materials were prohibited and people dressed to express their support or condemnation of political change. The men wore plain, dark clothing and wore their hair short and unpowdered in stark contrast to the pomp and grandeur of aristocratic powdered wigs.

The Directoire style – named after the Directory, the First French Republic – popularised the high waistline dresses and sleek silhouettes inspired by classical antiquity. However, the dress would take on a more imperial quality in years to come. In 1799, Napoleon overthrew the French government and went on to crown himself Emperor. At his coronation, his wife, Empress Josephine, achieved fashion icon status when she combined a high-waisted silk, white dress in neoclassical style with rich embroidery and an enormous diamond tiara. While heralding modernity, it was also a nod to the country's royal past, signifying luxury was acceptable again and symbolising Napoleon's ambitions for a new republic that was founded on liberty and freedom, but could also be regal and rich.

Englishwomen fell for Josephine's iconic style but the country's love affair with France was severely tested as Napoleon set his sights on conquering Britain. The Emperor was hell-bent on expanding his empire and by the early 19th century, Egypt and the majority of Continental Europe were under his control. Britain lived with the constant threat of invasion.

In 1802, the Treaty of Amiens instigated a period of peace but it was to prove short-lived for in 1803, Britain declared war on France. Over the next 12 years some of the most famous naval battles in history took place during the conflict between the two countries – these included the Battle of Trafalgar in 1805, when Lord Nelson's naval fleet defeated the French and Spanish, and the Peninsular War, where the UK assisted Spain and Portugal in control of the Iberian Peninsula. Napoleon was finally defeated in 1815 at the Battle of Waterloo by the Duke of Wellington's armies and his allies.

The years of intense fighting left a lasting impression on the era's fashions. One of the most popular and practical items in a lady's wardrobe was borne out of necessity. Throughout the early 1800s, there was a widespread outbreak among women of what became known as 'muslin disease' – spending too much time outdoors in freezing-cold temperatures wearing light, sheer fabrics meant that many of them perished from influenza and pneumonia. To prevent this, Regency women began wearing an outdoor Empire line, long-sleeved coat dress. Its origins lay in a form of uniform known as the pelisse and worn by Hussar mercenaries of Hungary of the 17th century. This short, fur-lined or fur-trimmed military jacket soon became popular in the cavalry units of armies across Europe.

The pelisse also became an indispensable item of women's clothing. In the spring and summer months, they were made of lightweight fabrics such as silk, satin or even muslin. In winter, they were framed with fur or swansdown. And as the Napoleonic Wars continued, they were festooned with frogging, decorative braids, cords, ropes of floss silk, tassels and trim, which were all accessories that featured on a soldier's uniform. The Spencer jacket – a short jacket with long sleeves and high neckline – was also embellished with military ornamental braids and fastenings. This extended to women's shawls too that were trimmed with ball fringe or more elaborate gold and silver thread embroideries.

After the success in Iberia, Spanish-inspired ornaments such as à la mamelouk sleeves – a long sleeve partitioned into five sections – added exotic flair to clothing. In a show of allegiance to the men fighting abroad, it became fashionable for women to resemble a member of the Hussars from the British Army.

The ostrich-feathered headdresses that the debutantes wear in court are also reminiscent of the shako – a military hat with a peak or plume – that was introduced into some Hussar regiments during the conflict. The outdoor conical hats that women wore were also inspired by these. However, the fashion for feathers at court was dictated less by modern-day trends and more by Queen Charlotte's strict fashion code – she was not a monarch to follow the fashions of the day and had no interest in becoming a style icon. This is reflected in her extravagant wigs and outfits throughout the show that represent the fashions of her youth and traditional order. A stickler for rules, Charlotte demanded that young women wear dresses with hoops or trains, so in reality, she would not have approved of the Empire-style dresses that the Featheringtons and Daphne choose for their presentation.

Styles in men's fashion were also heavily influenced by the military. Many elements of military, navy and army uniforms were added – the gold or gilt brass buttons and tasselled trims that the Bridgerton brothers wear on their three-piece suits and tailcoats are particularly in keeping with the time.

Hussar boots became a popular item of footwear for men. Inspired by those worn in the Army, they were calf-length with a pointed front upper. They were often worn with pantaloons or white breeches closely resembling what the soldiers would have worn in action. A versatile item, they could be worn during the day or evening for riding, sport and dancing. The tight-fitting design also provided an opportunity for men to show off their strong calves – which were a mark of virility – when promenading with a young lady or twirling her around the dancefloor.

Even the Napoleonic Wars couldn't destroy the English fascination with French culture and fashion, but in 1814, when the British could cross the Channel again, it was clear their fashion styles had diverged. The French ridiculed how low the waistlines of women's dresses had dropped in Britain to the point where the English quickly lifted them to be en vogue once again. Napoleon was finally defeated and peace restored, but Paris remained the leading fashion capital. And although Empress Josephine died in 1814, her style left a lasting impression and influence on the decades that followed.

Regency Fashion: Must-Know Terms for Budding Debutantes

Any woman of the Regency era worth her salt would be taught by her mama a whole range of terms and words she would need on visits to the modiste. Do you know your *sable* from your *plumper*? Would you be able to spot an *aigrette* from a *fichu*?

Let's start with **hose** – what we all know today, still, as women's stockings. But do you know of the term '**inexpressibles**'? This was used to describe men's trousers or breeches, especially tight-fitting ones!

After watching *Bridgerton*, you could be forgiven for thinking corsets were only for women. Not the case – a **Cumberland corset** was particularly popular with overweight dandies, similar to the Brummell bodice worn by the most celebrated dandy of all, Beau Brummell.

A society ever obsessed with modesty, Regency women were well-versed in the subtle art of the **tucker**, a piece of fabric that a lady would tuck into her bodice, thereby reducing the amount of cleavage on show to any budding suitors. To give an added swagger to any Regency lady, she might also have a **flounce** attached to her hem, a hand-pleated frill.

Today, we are well used to the idea of modifying our bodies, whether physically or using things like filters on social media. During the Regency era, elderly ladies and gentlemen had a form of this too – **plumpers** were artificial cheeks, placed inside the mouth to smooth facial contours.

To add an extra *je ne sais quoi* to an outfit, a lady might also opt for a **poke bonnet**, a hat with a brim that poked forward, useful in warding off unsuitable matches who got a little close . . .

A **sable** might also be a good option – fur from the highly prized marten, a weasel-like carnivore with brown or dark fur. Or perhaps a **frog** – a loop or gold braid fastening, used on military uniforms. Ladies would often wear them on their riding habits.

If you were attending a ball or court, you might spot an **aigrette** or two in the crowd. Feathers were a popular accompaniment to a fancy bash, by attaching them to a hat or wearing them as a headdress. The taller, the better!

And how could a tour through Regency fashion not include the **fichu**? Worn on the shoulders, this was a neckerchief, often in a triangular shape, made of muslin. Perhaps not as exciting as its name suggests!

Regency Hairstyles

The fashion for all things Roman and Grecian extended to men and women's hairstyles too. Powdered and pouffed-up constructions of the earlier Georgian period were now cast aside in favour of simpler, more elegant styles.

Women arranged their hair in soft curls around the face, with the rest of their hair scooped up into a chignon, plait or ponytail. If hair was left down, long curls would be left to trail over the back and shoulders. However, the 'natural' look actually took consider-able time and patience to achieve. Metal curling tongs or curl papers were a necessity for styles such as *à la medusa* (like Medusa, an icon of Greek mythology with snakes in place of hair) if you weren't naturally blessed with curls. Many upper-class ladies also had personal maids or dressers who could attend to their hair and help them achieve the fashionable looks of the day.

In the show, Daphne's delicate fringe and pin curls are inspired by Audrey Hepburn's iconic look in the 1956 film, *War and Peace*. Her swept-up hairdo signifies that she has left her childhood behind and is ready to marry. It also highlights her neck, which was believed to be the most elegant part of a woman's body.

During the Napoleonic Wars, travel to the Continent was no longer possible, so people sought solace and inspiration in their own gardens and the English countryside. The trend for women wearing flowers in their hair was influenced by Grecian and Roman statues, but also reflects an appreciation for nature and the great outdoors. Throughout the show, Marina Thompson's hair and outfits continually feature floral prints and accessories, which also signify the character's romantic love story.

There's no shortage of tiaras and hairpieces in *Bridgerton* and they are an historically accurate addition. During the Regency era, it was fashionable to wear them to formal occasions such as a ball. One of the show's more intricate designs is the hairpiece that the scheming Cressida Cowper wears to attract the attentions of the Prince. The character's obsession with status and hierarchy is reflected in the crown-shaped accessory sculpted out of wired braids, made complete with sewn-on pearls and threaded ribbons to match her ballgown.

The natural and tousled look was all the rage in men's hairstyles too. But styles such as the Windswept and the Brutus also took a lot of time and patience to cultivate. As head of the Bridgerton household and heir to the family fortune, Anthony is the obvious choice to channel a haircut inspired by a Roman senator. His bold sideburns and curled waves signify power and wealth. The Brutus was one of the most popular hairstyles of the era, championed by the innovative dresser of the day, Beau Brummell.

'Neckclothitania'

No matter how many brawls, duels or illicit tumbles Anthony Bridgerton gets embroiled in, you can always rely on his linen white neckcloth to stay as immaculate-looking as it was from the outset. It was King of the Dandies George Bryan Beau Brummell –

or simply 'Beau' – who took the necktie and turned it into the symbol of quintessential gentlemanly elegance we recognise today.

Beau prized understated simplicity and his sartorial taste for tailored dark coats, white linen shirts and long-length trousers laid the foundations for the modern standard three-piece suit. You would need the luxury of time to nail the look as perfectly as the celebrated dandy – young devotees of fashion would gather at his Mayfair apartment each morning to watch him take up to five hours to dress. Money would almost certainly come in handy too – Beau decreed the only way to achieve exquisitely shiny boots was to polish them with champagne. The ensemble could never be complete without the neckerchief as its crowning glory though – that alone could take up to two hours to tie.

In 1818, the neckerchief's popularity soared with the publication of 'Neckclothitania' – from the Napoleon to the Ballroom and the Horse Collar, the essay included all the different ways a gentleman could choose to arrange his neckcloth. Why not have a go and see how many styles you can master . . .

NECKCLOTHITANIA

Oriental — Mathematical — Osbaldeston

Napoleon — American — Mail Coach

Trone à Amour — Irish — Ball Room

Horse Collar — Hunting — Maharatta

Gordian Knot — Barrel Knot

Way of Folding

Pub⁴ by I.I. Stockdale. 4: Pall Mall. 1ˢᵗ Sept 1818.

Trone d'Amour Tie.*

The *trone d'Amour* is the most austere after the Oriental Tie — It must be extremely well stiffened with starch.† It is formed by one single horizontal dent in the middle. Color, *Yeux de fille en extase.*

Irish Tie.

This one resembles in some degree the Mathematical, with, however, this difference, that the horizontal indenture is placed *below* the point of junction formed by the collateral creases, instead of being above. The color, *Cerulean Blue.*

* So called from its resemblance to the Seat of Love.

† Starch is derived from the Teutonick word, "Stare" which means "stiff."

Ball Room Tie.

The Ball Room Tie when well put on, is quite delicious — It unites the qualities of the Mathematical and Irish, having two collateral dents and two horizontal ones, the one above as in the former, the other below as in the latter — It has no knot, but is fastened as the Napoleon. This should never of course be made with colors, but with the purest and most brilliant *blanc d'innocence virginale.*

Horse Collar Tie.

The Horse Collar has become, from some unaccountable reason, very universal. I can only attribute it to the inability of its wearers to make any other. It is certainly the worst and most vulgar, and I

133

Design your very own swoon-worthy *Bridgerton* outfits.

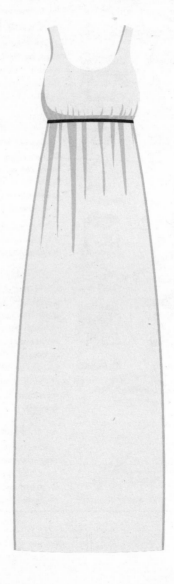

Chapter 8
Heartbeats Per Minute

Whether it's the thumping heartbeats of Daphne and Simon, the thundering hooves of Daphne's horse across Hyde Park, or Lady Danbury's impatiently tapping cane, each scene in the show has a pace and rhythm of its own that continually drives the plot forward. Let's not forget Anthony Bridgerton's intermittent energetic bouts of lovemaking either. But it's the ambitiously fresh musical score that intensifies the romance, drama and intrigue of so many of the series' most-loved and memorable scenes.

As well as the surge of interest in the Regency era's gowns and jewellery, viewers also fell in love with the imaginative classical reworkings of 21st-century pop hits that feature in the show. On release, the album *Bridgerton* (covers from the Netflix original series) went straight to number one in the Classical Albums Chart.

The two quartets who reinterpreted the contemporary songs are Vitamin String Quartet and Duomo. They feature on the album, along with Emmy award-winning composer Kris Bowers, who composed the main score for the show. Just as many of the show's costumes and set pieces borrow from, and blend, different periods, Bowers – with the help of executive producer Chris Van Dusen – wanted to create a sound that was 'classical but with a slightly modern approach' that was 'still romantic'.

It was music supervisor Alexandra Patsavas who came up with the idea of using the quartet covers as the backdrop to some of the series' most memorable moments. So, what songs did she choose and what extra meaning do they give to the scenes?

'Thank U, Next' – Ariana Grande, performed by Vitamin String Quartet

This plays as Anthony takes Daphne for 'a turn about the room' during the first ball of the season, while debutantes waltz in the background. As they promenade, he dismisses each and every suitor vying for his sister's attention, explaining the reasons for their unsuitability and why she must keep moving on to the next, and the next, and the next. To begin with, Daphne is a wide-eyed, naive debutante, but the song hints at her burgeoning power and the freedom she will have to choose whom she loves. By the time she leaves the ball, all the suitors are left wanting more.

'Girls Like You' – Maroon 5, performed by Vitamin String Quartet

In this scene, Marina Thompson appears to have taken the limelight away from Daphne as a string of suitors hurry to her drawing room the morning after the ball, intent on winning her favour. In the original song, Cardi B raps a message of empowerment over the melody that declares her superiority over all the other girls. Marina has her moment in the sun, but the tables soon turn when she finds herself at the mercy of a society that punishes women for their sexual autonomy.

'In My Blood' – Shawn Mendes, performed by Vitamin String Quartet

This plays during a crucial scene at the end of Episode 2 when Daphne and Simon dance together at a ball. Simon asks Daphne to call him by his first name and it's clear that their faux relationship is developing into something genuine and heartfelt. As he gives her up to another suitor, he watches from the sidelines and realises their bond is strengthening. For the first time we sense his vulnerability and fear of being alone: as Simon grows more attached to Daphne, can he really face a life without her?

'Bad Guy' – Billie Eilish, performed by Vitamin String Quartet

This plays while the couple continue to perform in front of the ton. Simon pretends to erupt in anger when Daphne agrees to dance with yet another dandy. But beneath the pretence their true attachment continues to grow. Will Simon put his rakish days far behind him and allow himself to fall in love?

'Strange' – Celeste, covered by Kris Bowers

Kris Bowers reinterpreted Celeste's jazz and soul-fused ballad with cellist Hillary Smith for the wedding night scene we were all waiting to get behind. It's the moment when Daphne and Simon finally bare all and consummate their relationship. The main melody conveys their longing and desire for each other and the euphoria they feel when they finally release the emotions they've been suppressing. It's the perfect song to let your loved one know they set your heart alight.

'Wildest Dreams' – Taylor Swift, performed by Duomo

Once Daphne and Simon have got their night at the coach inn out of the way, there's no stopping them. This cover of Taylor Swift's huge hit provides the backdrop to the show's most memorable romp montage or 'bonk-age'. With the various rooms and grounds of Clyvedon Castle available to them, the couple are free to be as wild as they want, wherever they choose.

Historically-suited pieces by Haydn, Beethoven and Mozart also feature throughout the show, but Max Richter's modern reworking of Vivaldi's *Four Seasons* in the final episode of the series is particularly memorable. It's an uplifting and joyous piece of music that perfectly accompanies the rain scene during the last ball of the season.

Chapter 9

Dances to Master

As Shakira once sang, the 'hips don't lie'. It's an adage that rings true for many of the popular dances of the Regency era, even if the moves were a lot less vigorous than we're used to in more contemporary times. From fastening button cuffs to random jealous outbursts at balls and other events, Daphne and Simon put on a masterful charade to fool society into believing they're a couple, but the falsities melt away on the dancefloor. When the couple dance together for the first time at the Vauxhall Pleasure Gardens, their burgeoning feelings for each other are impossible to hide. The other guests at the ball look on agape, mesmerised by the obvious connection between the pair – including, of course, Lady

Whistledown, who describes the match as the best of the season.

Indeed, dancing was about the only chance a couple had to escape the watchful eye of a chaperone and indulge in any kind of flirtation. With dancing came a rare opportunity for intimacy, not least the thrilling prospect of actually touching hands. In *Bridgerton*, Daphne also uses the two minutes of twirling to quiz her dancing partners on their preferences to find out if they're a suitable match.

The stakes were pretty high when it came to dancing. A clumsy dancer could put off a potential suitor or kill any initial attraction stone dead so as well as being accomplished at needlework, pianoforte and foreign languages, it was essential that ladies in high society mastered the moves of the day too. The etiquette and fashion manual – *The Mirror of Graces* – described dancing as an 'effective exhibition' for showcasing beauty and displaying 'fine form, elegant taste, and graceful carriage to advantage'. No pressure then.

It was important for men to master the latest dance moves too. The Duke of Wellington was adamant that all his officers could dance and the British statesman Lord Chesterfield once wrote that although dancing was 'very trifling' and 'silly', it was also 'one of those established follies to which people of sense are sometimes obliged to conform, and then they should be able to do it well'.

Help was on hand and no debutante would be sent out into society until she was deemed ready to demonstrate grace, musicality and mastery of the most popular dances of the day. Well-known socialites of the time, such as Lady Caroline Lamb and the Duchess of Devonshire, organised morning classes in their homes, where dancing masters or 'caper merchants' taught young women the more intricate steps and sequences. The more steps you were able to effortlessly perform, the more time and attention you could give to impressing your partner with your sparkling wit.

For anyone who balked under the pressure at a ball, help was also on hand with crib sheets. Dancers could carry a fan with the latest dances printed on it, or on a ribbon worn about their wrist or even snuck into a reticule. With the rise of print, instruction manuals became increasingly popular, with illustrations and hints on how to retain dignity and decorum while moving around the dancefloor.

The Regency Dances to Master

The English Country Dance

Popular since the 17th century, this communal dance was energetic, light-hearted, fun and easy to get the hang of, no matter how many whiskys you might have swilling around in you. Also known as the Long Dance, it allowed for a large number of dancers in each set. Partners faced each other in a line and performed a sequence of distinct moves from the top to the bottom. The dances were set to traditional, upbeat and universally loved numbers such as 'Lady Townsend's Whim', 'The Duke of York's Cotillion' and 'Lady Salisbury's Fancy'.

Cotillion

One of English novelist Jane Austen's favourite dances, the cotillion was another form of lively, social country dance for four couples. Although it normally began with a circle, most of the dance was performed in a square, with various changes that allowed partners to swap. Originating from France, so many of the cotillions kept their French names, such as 'La Boulanger'. The dance incorporated a variety of elaborate moves that included the 'Allemande' – where partners interlaced their arms – and the 'Promenade' – where couples joined hands and travelled across or within the set of dancers.

Quadrille

Quadrille dancing evolved out of the cotillion and was particularly popular across London's ballrooms from the mid-1810s. It was different to the cotillion in that the dance flowed from one lead couple to the next, omitting moves such as the promenade. Many French quadrilles were danced by just two couples, who remained together throughout the set. Some of the steps such as the jeté and chassé involved a variety of leaps, hops and pliés that were particularly tricky to perform correctly, let alone elegantly.

The Waltz

Waltz music, characterised by the 3/4 signature, had been popular in country dances since the mid-18th century. But it couldn't be further from the waltz dance for couples, which was a radical break from the traditional moves performed in sets. Indeed, when it was first brought to British shores, the waltz was to scandalise the dancefloors of Regency Britain. Aside from the fact that the couple were in such close proximity, there were fears that all the turning could result in ladies becoming dizzy and losing their self-control. Could this be the real reason why Daphne becomes so smitten with the Duke after she waltzes with him?

In 1815, the waltz was finally introduced to the high society club Almack's – it had been banned there for a number of years. Once endorsed in London's most exclusive venue, however, its popularity spread across the city. But the waltz still met with resistance from some quarters. In 1816, the Prince Regent included the waltz at one of his balls. A few days later, a piece was published in *The Times* condemning his choice:

'We remarked with pain that the indecent foreign dance called the Waltz was introduced (we believe for the first time) at the English court on Friday last . . . it is quite sufficient to cast one's eyes on the voluptuous intertwining of the limbs and close compressure on the bodies in their dance, to see that it is indeed far removed from the modest reserve which has hitherto been considered distinctive of English females. . . .'

Luckily, no one took much notice of *The Times*, not least the modest English females who were eager to embrace the latest dance craze. In 1816, dance master Thomas Wilson published *A Description of the Correct Method of Waltzing*. It included his illustration of the nine positions of the waltz, none of which look even remotely shocking. Well, not by today's standards at least.

Famous waltzes*

- 'Valzer dei Fiori' (*The Nutcracker*) – Tchaikovsky
- 'Swan Lake Waltz' (*Swan Lake*) – Tchaikovsky
- 'Grande Valse Villageoise' (*The Sleeping Beauty*) – Tchaikovsky
- 'Masquerade Suite Waltz' – Aram Khachaturian
- 'Slavonic Dance, Op. 72, No. 2' – Antonín Dvořák
- 'Wiener Blut, Op. 354' – Johann Strauss II

---

*www.vogue.co.uk/arts-and-lifestyle/article/bridgerton-soundtrack

Chapter 10
Pioneering Women

Although Daphne Bridgerton delights as the 'Diamond of the First Water', her sister Eloise is equally fascinating. Her witty and perceptive observations, highlighting the frustrations and hypocrisies of Regency society, drew a legion of devoted fans to her. Throughout the show, she laments women's inferior standing, their lack of freedoms and the fact that their achievements are reduced to how pretty they look or how fashionable their hair is.

For Eloise, it would be a worthy accomplishment to stretch herself intellectually and attend university. This would not become an option for women until the latter half of the 19th century and even then, it was incredibly rare. At the age of 17, Eloise is expected to enter society rather than follow her dream of becoming an author. No wonder she craves the freedoms her brothers have.

Although they're not mentioned in the TV series, Eloise would have delighted in the company of the Bluestocking Society, a club for clever ladies and their gentlemen friends. Founded in the 1750s, it represented modern, intellectual women who favoured 'rational conversation' as a means to progress society, rather than conform to the stifling social mores women had to abide by. Its founding members were the aristocrat Elizabeth Montagu – highly regarded for her witty repartee – and the Irish-born scholar and poet Elizabeth Vesey.

The society became highly regarded for attracting some of the most accomplished and learned women of the day – members included the classicist and translator Elizabeth Carter, the first British female historian Catharine Macaulay, poet Anna Seward and the educator, social reformer and abolitionist Hannah More.

Contrary to popular belief, the society was open to males, among them the English writer Samuel Johnson and botanist, translator and author Benjamin

Stillingfleet. Many of its members faced ridicule and condemnation from politicians such as Robert Walpole, as well as some Romantic literary male figures. Despite this, the group paved the way for many other women to pursue their ambitions and be regarded in their field as intellectual equals to men. Described below are just some of the incredible Regency females who left an indelible mark on science, history, culture and the arts.

Mary Shelley

Mary Wollstonecraft Shelley (née Godwin) was a teenager when she eloped with the romantic poet Percy Bysshe Shelley. It caused huge controversy at the time and the pair were alienated from polite society, even after they married. While holidaying in Geneva, with Percy and Lord Byron, Mary wrote her seminal masterpiece, *Frankenstein*, thought to be the world's first ever science fiction book. It was published anonymously in 1818 and many people assumed her husband had written it. Shelley went on to write more plays, books and poems, and supported herself financially from writing throughout her life.

Dr James Barry (Margaret Ann Bulkley)

Born in Cork, southern Ireland, Margaret Ann Bulkley was known as female in childhood but disguised herself as a man to pursue a career in medicine. After graduating, she joined the British Army and practised medicine all over the British Empire. In 1826, she performed the first successful Caesarean section (C-section) by a European doctor in Cape Town. She went on to become Inspector-General of Hospitals and vastly improved health conditions for soldiers and indigenous people. Her true identity wasn't uncovered until after she died in 1865. The discovery rocked Victorian society.

Anna Atkins

Anna Atkins had an avid interest in botany and illustrated her father John George Children's books on shells (he invented a method to extract silver from ore without the need for mercury). After marrying John Pelly Atkins in 1825, Anna continued to pursue her scientific interests and learnt about early forms of chemical photography developed by Royal Society members William Henry Fox Talbot and Sir John Herschel. In 1842, she self-published the first part of a work with photographic images – *Photographs of British Algae: Cyanotype Impression*. Her innovative techniques blended art and science to create beautifully detailed blueprints of botanical specimens.

Etheldred Benett

Born in Wiltshire, Etheldred Benett began studying and collecting fossils in 1810. The eldest daughter of landed gentry, she had her own money and never married. She built up a vast collection of fossils that she discovered throughout the south-west of England and contributed extensively to the science of fossils. Benett is credited as being the first female geologist, gaining recognition all over the world – Tsar Alexander I granted her an honorary doctorate in civil law from St Petersburg University without realising she was a woman.

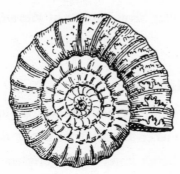

Harriet Mellon

Born to a wardrobe keeper in a travelling theatre company, British actress Mellon rose up the ranks of high society to become senior partner of Coutts Bank and a duchess to boot. Born in 1777, she made her acting debut as a young woman at London's Drury Lane Theatre, where she went on to play a variety of comic roles and was an understudy to leading actress of the day, tragedienne Sarah Siddons.

It was here that she attracted the attention of the wealthy banker Thomas Coutts, founder of Coutts & Co, whom she married in 1815. After his death in 1822, she became extremely wealthy, inheriting his estate and a 50 per cent stake in the bank. She took an active role in the bank's management and proved to have excellent business acumen. When she remarried in 1827, to William Beauclerk, 9th Duke of St Albans, she asked Walter Scott, author of *Waverley*, to write her life story.

Caroline Herschel

The German-born astronomer was the first woman in England to receive a salary for her work in science, assisting her better-known older brother – Friedrich

Wilhelm Herschel KH, FRS. In 1786, she became the first woman to discover a comet and over the next 11 years, she discovered seven others. In 1828, Caroline was the first woman to be awarded a Gold Medal of the Royal Astronomical Society. In 1835, she was named an Honorary Member of the Royal Astronomical Society. She was also an accomplished singer, who performed in her brother's concerts.

Mary Linwood

Artist Mary Linwood was an educator who achieved great success and recognition for her exceptional needlework. Her specialty was producing full-sized copies of famous great works of art in crewel wool. She came to fame after her first London exhibition in 1787, which was the first art show to be illuminated by gaslight.

In 1790, she received a medal from the Society of Arts. Mary also met most of the crowned heads of Europe – she was invited to Windsor Castle by Queen Charlotte and is said to have created Napoleon's portrait from life. She embroidered her last piece at the age of 78 and kept working as a school mistress until a year before her death at the age of 90.

Mary Fairfax Somerville

Scottish scientist, writer and polymath Mary Fairfax Somerville showed huge academic potential from a young age. At 13, she was sent to writing school in Edinburgh, where she studied arithmetic. Back at home, she read Shakespeare voraciously and taught herself Latin. She was largely self-taught and stayed up late to study books on algebra and geometry.

In 1804, Mary married her first husband, Samuel Greig. The pair had two sons. Upon Samuel's death, three years after their marriage, Mary's inheritance enabled her to pursue her academic interests. She began to solve mathematical problems and had several of these published in the mathematical repository. Her studies extended to astronomy, chemistry, geography, microscopy and magnetism.

In 1812, Mary re-married, to William Somerville. He encouraged her studies and together, they met and befriended many leading figures of the day, such as J. M. W. Turner and Walter Scott. In 1826, she published her first paper exploring the relationship between light and magnetism, in the Proceedings of the Royal Society.

Somerville went on to translate Pierre-Simon Laplace's *Le Mécanique Céleste* (The Mechanism of the Heavens), which became a set textbook for under-graduates at Cambridge until the 1880s. She produced an expanded version with her own explanation of the mathematics behind the workings of the solar system. The work made her famous and Sir David Brewster, inventor of the kaleidoscope, described her as 'the most extraordinary woman in Europe'.

Mary was a great advocate for women's equality and started a school for girls from the middle and lower classes. She also tutored Lord Byron's daughter Augusta – better known as Ada Lovelace – whose pioneering work contributed greatly to the field of computer science.

Maria Hester Park (née Reynolds)

Little is known about Maria Hester Park's life but she was one of the most prolific 18th-century women composers. Born in 1760, she gave public performances on the piano and harpsichord in a series of concerts, in venues across London.

After marriage to Thomas Park in 1787, she ended her career as a performer but went on to compose for the next 25 years, up until her death. Mozart influenced many of her sonatas and she sent several of her pieces to Haydn. She also taught piano to many members of the aristocracy, including Georgiana, Duchess of Devonshire and her daughters.

Chapter 11
Codes and Conventions

Despite the strict codes and conventions governing society during the Georgian era, the period has been described by historians as one of the most permissive in British history. Men and women across all classes and hierarchies revelled in the masquerades of the pleasure gardens, where disguise provided ample opportunities to play with gender roles and enjoy a series of illicit encounters.

Members of le bon ton tolerated affairs – as long as they weren't paraded in public – and aristocrats, such as Lady Elizabeth Foster, brought up her two illegitimate children in a ménage à trois with her lover, the Duke of Devonshire, and his wife, her close friend Georgiana.

Attitudes towards gender weren't as fixed or prescribed as they became in the Victorian era. Whig

Party leader Charles James Fox openly enjoyed dressing up in high-heeled red shoes, brightly coloured fabrics and wearing a blue-tinted hairstyle – a style synonymous with the Macaronis, who 'exceeded the ordinary bounds of fashion' by dressing in effeminate and outrageous fashions. The Irish actress Peg Woffington was also celebrated for her comedic travesty role, playing the character of Sir Harry Wildair in *The Constant Couple*. However, by the late 1790s, George III was so concerned about the morality of his subjects that he established the Proclamation Society Against Vice and Immorality to prosecute those guilty of 'dissolute, immoral, or disorderly practices'. It had little impact on the majority of fun-loving Georgians' exploits, but the consequences for the gay community in Georgian society would be dire.

Molly Houses

As Lord Wetherby tells Benedict Bridgerton in the TV series, it takes great courage and risk for him to defy society's traditional expectations. As a gay man, he must hide his relationship with artist Henry Granville at all costs or run the risk of the severest punishment. Homosexuality was not only illegal in the British

Empire, but also carried the possibility of a death sentence.

Gay men sought refuge in underground clubs and bars that became known as 'Molly Houses' – 'Molly' being slang for a gay man (possibly from the Latin word *mollis*, for soft or effeminate). Set up in brandy shops, taverns or theatres across the city of London, men could meet in Molly Houses to socialise and have sex. In these spaces, gay subculture could thrive – to a certain degree. It was common for men to wear women's clothes and adopt typically feminine personas. 'Duchess of Camomile', 'Plump Nelly', 'Aunt May' and 'Susan Guzzle' were among the pseudonyms they gave each other.

Certain districts of the city became known as Molly hotspots – Moorfields, Lincoln's Inn and Covent Garden. The south side of Finsbury Square was a popular cruising area known as Sodomites Walk. Some public toilets and parks were known as 'Molly Markets'.

The Vere Street Coterie

In 1810, The White Swan, which provided a variety of attractions for homosexual men, was opened by James

Cook and a man known only as 'Yardley'. The basement had a bedroom complete with a lady's dressing room. It even included a makeshift chapel, where the Reverend John Church reportedly performed the first same-sex wedding ceremonies ever to take place in the country. Within six months, the place was raided by the Bow Street Runners, London's first professional police force, as part of George III's crackdown. Twenty-seven men were arrested. Most of them were released because they were able to pay large enough bribes to the police. Those who couldn't afford to do so remained in custody.

While Yardley escaped, James Cook was charged for running a disorderly house. Two of the men arrested were sentenced to prison, while another six were sentenced to an hour in the pillory, a wooden or metal device on a post with holes for securing the head and hands. A vicious mob gathered around to pelt them with anything they could lay their hands on – including, reportedly, dead cats. Cook was almost unconscious by the end and they were all seriously injured. The Vere Street Coterie – as it became known – was reported in every newspaper. It unleashed a wave of fresh accusations against members of the clergy and prominent politicians – Lord Castlereagh killed himself after a blackmail campaign began against him. Two army officers implicated in the scandal were brought to trial on charges of sodomy and subsequently convicted and sentenced to death. The harsh crackdown and punishments terrorised the gay community and many escaped to France, which had a freer and more tolerant attitude towards homosexuality.

The Ladies of Llangollen

As women were less able to achieve financial security without a husband, the majority of lesbians in Georgian society married and carried out their relationships in secret. If they were discovered, legal action was typically not taken against them.

Eleanor Butler and Sarah Ponsonby were two upper-class women from Ireland, who refused to end up in loveless, arranged marriages. In 1780, they left County Kilkenny in the south-east of the country and moved to a cottage in the village of Llangollen in Wales. The pair attracted many curious visitors and admirers that included William Wordsworth, Lady Caroline Lamb and Lord Byron. The Duke of Wellington paid them a visit too, on his travels between Dublin and London.

There's no conclusive proof that Eleanor and Sarah's relationship was sexual. They both adamantly denied it when this was suggested by a publication, although this is hardly surprising, given the repercussions they might have faced. The two women lived a modest lifestyle with the help of their relatives and friends. Queen Charlotte, who was fascinated by them, persuaded George III to grant them a pension and Wordsworth wrote a sonnet about them, 'To the Lady E.B. and the Hon. Miss P'.

They lived in Llangollen for 50 years and are buried together in a church in the village.

Anne Lister

The Ladies of Llangollen are said to have inspired Anne Lister – now regarded as 'the first modern lesbian' – to informally marry her lover, Ann Walker.

Lister was fortunate enough to inherit enough wealth and land – she inherited Shibden Hall in West Yorkshire – to live independently without ever marrying a man. She was known to locals as 'Gentleman Jack', always dressing in black and refusing to follow fashionable female trends of the day.

Lister was a successful businesswoman, who opened a colliery and owned shares in the canal and railway industries. She kept a personal diary throughout her life, which gives fascinating information about social, political and economic events of the time. The diaries also include intimate accounts of her love affairs with other women – many of whom were married. These sections were written in a code she created from Greek and Latin, mathematical symbols, punctuation and the Zodiac.

In 1834, Lister and Walker exchanged sacred vows in Holy Trinity Church, Goodramgate, York – the building now hosts a commemorative plaque. The couple lived together at Shibden Hall until Lister died in 1840.

Chapter 12
Location, Location, Location

From the elegant, well-lit townhouses of Mayfair to Queen Charlotte's magnificent royal court, Regency London is at the heart of all the main action in *Bridgerton*. However, in reality, very few locations in modern-day London featured at all. Instead, some of the finest stately homes across the north and south-west of England were chosen to provide the backdrop for the show's key homes and residences.

So, before you plan your own Grand Tour of classical antiquities across Europe to rival Colin Bridgerton's gap year, take a whistle-stop tour of some of the country's very own historic treasures. We can't promise you'll be received for tea in Violet Bridgerton's drawing room or spot the Duke prowling the corridors of his country estate, but you'll have the chance to see where some of the show's most memorable scenes took place and soak up some beautiful scenery in the process. And if you're a real lady of leisure, why not take seven months out for a proper exploration? That's the amount of time it took for the cast and crew of builders, painters and prop-makers to construct and shoot the entire first season.

Wilton House

Wilton House is a Palladian country house set in beautiful Wiltshire countryside, near Salisbury. With over 22 acres of parkland and gardens, it is bordered by the Rivers Wylye and Nadder, and has been home to the Earls of Pembroke since the 1540s. Although a priory stood on the site from the year 871, the majority of the present house was built in the mid-16th century and is based on original designs by the architect Inigo Jones. Palladian in style, the lavishly decorated state rooms house a world-famous art collection that includes Pieter Brueghel, Rembrandt van Rijn and Richard Wilson.

The home's Double Cube room features one of its most highly prized works of art – Anthony van Dyck's portrait of the Earl, 'Philip Herbert and his family'. An enormous piece of artwork – almost 17 feet wide and 11 deep – that dominates the majority of the west wall, it is this room that was chosen as the setting for one of the most pivotal scenes in the show – the presentation of the debutantes at Queen Charlotte's Court in St James's Palace.

The stakes for these young women were incredibly high. Not only did elite members of the ton gather to survey the season's new crop of high society ladies, their 'performance' – which hinged on how well they could curtsy in front of the monarch – was subsequently reported on by the press. It was vital they made a good impression during their formal debut as it improved their chances of being introduced to wealthy and well-connected men. A debutante was considered to be particularly successful if she secured an engagement within the first season.

Tight corset or not, it's little wonder Prudence Featherington faints under the pressure. Daphne, however, remains far more composed and makes a 'flawless' impression upon the Queen. Before too long, Lady Whistledown has given her the coveted title – 'Incomparable of the Season'.

As was the case with the Bridgertons, many aristocratic families of the time did have genuine royal connections. In the late 18th century, one of the rooms at Wilton House was converted for King George III and Queen Charlotte. They both visited the house to inspect British troops preparing to fight in the American War of Independence.

With so many lavish rooms to choose from, the estate also proved perfect for a number of different residences in the show – it served as the Duke's London home, 'Hastings House', as well as the dining room at Clyvedon Castle and Lady Danbury's drawing room and grand hall. The grounds of Wilton House were also used to recreate Hyde Park, while its Palladian bridge and 19th-century Italian garden appear in several of the outdoor scenes.

What other films and TV shows have been shot here? *Mrs Brown* (1997), *Johnny English* (2003), *The Crown* (Netflix, 2016–) and *Pride and Prejudice* (BBC, 1995).

The Royal Crescent and No. 1 Royal Crescent
Built between 1767 and 1775, the Royal Crescent in the world heritage city of Bath was designed by John

Wood the Younger. It remains one of the greatest examples of Georgian architecture in the UK.

Thirty Grade I-listed terraced houses make up the sweeping crescent, which provides the perfect spot to take in stunning views across Royal Victoria Park and the surrounding countryside.

For those who know Bath well, the Royal Crescent is instantly recognisable as one of the city's most unique and well-loved landmarks. But for the show, it doubles as Mayfair's Grosvenor Square – one of the most prestigious and exclusive addresses in Regency London. Built between 1720–25, the square formed the centrepiece for an eight-acre estate development. This area became increasingly sought after as the upper classes looked to rent, or buy, residences west of the city that were closer to Hyde Park, Parliament at Westminster and the Court of St James.

Throughout the remainder of the 18th century, hundreds of villas, mansions and townhouses were built with symmetrical columns and façades inspired by classical antiquity. By the time of the Regency, Mayfair was home to many of the ton's most affluent and powerful families. W1 remains one of the most exclusive and highly-sought-after areas of London.

Today, No. 1 Royal Crescent is a Regency museum that showcases historic furniture, pictures and objects, capturing how families lived during the Georgian period. The exterior is used for the home of the Featherington family. Part of the Royal Crescent also serves as the London home of Siena Rosso, the opera singer who hits all the right notes for Anthony Bridgerton. As Siena laments, the couple can only demonstrate their love in 'darkness, not the light' and this is one of the places he visits her in the evening – away from the prying eyes of high society that would deem their relationship to be far too improper.

What other films and TV shows have been shot here? *The Duchess* (2008), *Persuasion* (2008), *Catch Us If You Can* (1965) and *The Elusive Pimpernel* (BBC mini-series, 1969).

The Holburne Museum

This is another building in Bath's long list of Georgian gems that was inspired by classical antiquity. Designed by Sir Reginald Blomfield RA, it was built of Bath stone between 1795–96 and was originally intended as a place for people to gather socially and enjoy local afternoon tea, before promenading in the nearby pleasure gardens.

Sir William Holburne (1704–71), who lived in a nearby crescent, was an avid collector of art, sculpture, porcelain and Roman antiquities. After he died, his sister, Mary Anne Barbara Holburne, bequeathed his collection to the people of Bath. In 1893 it became the city's first art gallery. Today, the Holburne Museum boasts a strong selection of English 18th-century portraits, including five by Thomas Gainsborough.

In the show, the building's elegant façade and beautiful gardens were used as the exterior for Lady Danbury's home.

What other films and TV shows have been shot here? *Vanity Fair* (2004), *The Duchess* (2008) and *The Count of Monte Cristo* (BBC, 1964).

Bath Assembly Rooms

Yet another of Bath's beloved tourist spots features in the show. Like the Royal Crescent, it was designed by John Wood the Younger in 1769. The assembly was intended to be a place for dancing and music and comprised four rooms – the Great Octagon, Tea Room, Ball Room and Card Room.

After it first opened in 1771 with a grand ball, the Bath Assembly Rooms soon became a much-frequented haunt for some of the most notable figures in fashionable society – the writers Jane Austen and Charles Dickens to name but a few.

The glamorous ballroom provides the perfect setting for the first social event of the season – Lady Danbury's ball – where every young woman yearns to attract the eye of an eligible suitor. It's here that Daphne Bridgerton and Simon Basset enjoy their first encounter, if only by chance, due to Lord Berbrooke's persistent advances. Their inaugural tête-à-tête may be a little terse but from the outset, the chemistry is evidently as electrifying as a nocturnal light display at Vauxhall's Pleasure Gardens.

Temple of Venus, Stowe Landscape Gardens

Between 1730 and 1748, the architect William Kent created a set of stunning Palladian-inspired temples in the gardens of Stowe House in Buckinghamshire. The Temple of Venus features four busts that represent Cleopatra, Faustina, Nero and Vespasian, who were all known for their pleasure-seeking pursuits. No wonder it was chosen as the setting for Vauxhall Pleasure Gardens in London. Throughout the 18th and 19th centuries, pleasure gardens were outdoor spaces dedicated to music, dancing and art. They featured fireworks, illuminations and operas. Perhaps most risqué of all were the masquerades where, with their identities hidden, affluent members of Georgian society weren't above indulging in some pretty scandalous behaviour.

Of course, it would still be improper for any well-to-do lady to be caught on her own in the gardens without a chaperone. But it's here that Daphne finds herself alone and fending off the unwanted attentions of Lord Berbrooke. As Simon rushes to her defence, she floors Berbrooke with a right hook that both surprises and impresses the Duke.

The pair's first dance is pictured on the Temple of Venus and it's during this scene that they plot to keep the ambitious mamas at bay and bring a slew of impressive suitors to Daphne's door. As Simon instructs her to look into his eyes, like she really means it, we get the first inkling that she sure isn't faking.

What other films and TV shows have been shot here? *The Crown* (Netflix, 2016–), *X-Men: First Class* (2011) and *Indiana Jones and the Last Crusade* (1989).

Castle Howard

Described as the jewel in North Yorkshire's crown, this grand sweeping estate near York boasts the largest dome in a private residence and took 100 years to build. It even has its own glittering replica of the Crown Jewels. Home to the Howard family for 300 years, its royal connections go back to Charles II, who bestowed the first Earldom of Carlisle on Charles Howard in the year of his coronation. It was the epic ITV television series *Brideshead Revisited* that first made this estate famous, back in 1981. Since then, the incomparable structure and stunning surrounding landscape continue to make it an extremely popular choice for location scouts.

Bridgerton fans may be disappointed to learn that the Duke's country house, Clyvedon Castle, doesn't actually exist in real life – but Castle Howard's regal splendour makes it the perfect dwelling place for a man with title.

It's not until the sixth episode of the series that we get the opportunity to take in the breathtaking sights this private residence has to offer or witness some of the steamiest love scenes between Daphne and Simon. The vast expanse of Castle Howard's grounds, with its glittering lakes and rolling hills, provide the pair with an inordinate amount of options for their al fresco trysts, as well as the opportunity to be as vocal as they choose – lest any curious servants are prowling the corridors. One of their most passionate love scenes was filmed at the Temple of Four Winds, which is located at the Temple Terrace in Castle Howard. Originally used as a place for 'refreshment and reading', books were certainly not at the forefront of their minds on this occasion.

What else has been filmed here? *Lady L* (1965), *Barry Lyndon* (1975), *Brideshead Revisited* (ITV, 1981), *Death Comes to Pemberley* (BBC mini-series, 2013), *Victoria* (ITV, 2016–) and Arctic Monkeys' *Four Out Of Five* music video (2018).

Ranger's House

A hidden gem in Greenwich, south-east London, Ranger's House is one of the least well-known spots of *Bridgerton*'s shooting locations. However, its fame has now surely rocketed as the red-brick façade will be forever recognised as Bridgerton House – the Bridgerton family's main city residence.

The Georgian red-brick villa was built in 1723 by Captain Francis Hosier (Vice-Admiral of the Blue in the Royal Navy) to give him easy access to the Thames. Over the years, it has also been home to English royalty and aristocracy. In 1813, the year that *Bridgerton* is set, the house was occupied by King George III's elder sister, Princess Augusta, and between 1806–14, the Prince Regent's wife Caroline, Princess of Wales, lived next door in Montagu House after separating from her husband. It was here that she threw parties reported to rival his wild and outrageous exploits. The house is now home to the Wernher Collection and features more than 700 objects of fine and decorative art.

In the show, Bridgerton House is also notable for the luscious wisteria that climbs its façade. However, in real life this isn't normally there. One of the crew's toughest challenges was planting and dismantling a wisteria tree to cover the family home. Happily, they were able to make use of it in other scenes, such as the Queen's Garden Party.

RAF Hilton

None of the family scenes inside Bridgerton House were actually filmed at Ranger's House. For these, the crew used RAF Hilton, a Royal Air Force station in Buckinghamshire, which has been used by the military since 1913. Although not Georgian, the interior offered sufficient space to create the Grand Hall, stairs, hallway and smoking room of Bridgerton House. It's here that Eloise Bridgerton screams at the top of her lungs in exasperation as her family wait for her elder sister Daphne to make her first appearance before she is presented at court.

Lady Trowbridge's ball was also filmed at Hatfield House and its gardens are home to the maze, where one of the most highly-charged moments between Daphne and Simon takes place. During the ball, Daphne awkwardly sidesteps the advances of her new beau, Prince Frederick of Prussia. As they dance, she realises she can no longer ignore her true feelings for the Duke, no matter how many beautiful diamond necklaces the Prince wraps around her neck. She runs out onto the terrace and tears off the necklace. After a heated exchange with Simon, she runs into the maze and he follows her. It's here that they finally embrace and share their first kiss, unable to suppress the sparks flying between them.

Unfortunately, the maze is part of the private West Garden at Hatfield House so it's unlikely you'll be able to re-enact your own amorous encounter there. However, you can still catch a glimpse of it from the terrace.

What other films and TV shows have been filmed here? *The Queen* (2006), *Flyboys* (2006), *Diana: Last Days of a Princess* (TLC docudrama, 2007) and *The King's Speech* (2010).

The butterflies and the bees

Did you spot these symbols for the rival families in the show?

Production designer Will Hughes-Jones wanted to create colour palettes that reflected the differences between the Bridgerton and Featherington families. Wedgewood blue is the predominant shade that features throughout the Bridgertons' home and is matched to their outfits throughout the series. It symbolises the classical and traditional sensibilities of family and reflects that they are established, represent old money and are at the top of the social hierarchy. In contrast, the Featheringtons' home is decorated with more garish and ostentatious colours, such as bright greens and yellows, that represent their desire to be noticed and move higher up the social strata. This is also reflected in the outfits that Portia Featherington and her three daughters wear – throughout the show, their taste – or lack thereof – is regularly commented on.

The butterfly motif also appears on the family's outfits, as well as their headpieces and necklaces – one of the most memorable costumes of the show being Penelope Featherington's yellow ballgown. They also appear throughout the family's home – anyone with eagle eyes might have spotted the 600 metal butterflies fixed to their grand staircase. Symbolically, they represent the family's desire to transform the way they are seen in society.

Throughout the series, bees feature regularly as a motif on the outfits and headpieces worn by the Bridgertons. They bookend the beginning and finale of the show – one appears on the Bridgertons' doorknocker and the windowsill of Daphne's birthing chamber. The bee symbolises fertility, abundance and teamwork, as well as Daphne's ascension to Duchess through good and fair means.

Glossary

Find the words in the wordsearch:

BLUESTOCKING ☐
VISCOUNT ☐
SWOON ☐
COURSES ☐
DUKE ☐
DUNDERHEAD ☐
VULGAR ☐
DIAMOND ☐
MODISTE ☐
SIRE ☐
DUCHESS ☐
TON ☐
RAKE ☐
FLAWLESS ☐
NONESUCH ☐
DEBUTANTE ☐
SNUFF ☐
FACER ☐

O	U	I	N	O	O	W	S	F	U	T	H	E	I
H	D	C	N	T	V	I	S	C	O	U	N	T	S
C	E	O	S	D	W	N	B	S	T	W	W	T	N
R	B	U	B	U	E	O	L	N	O	N	S	S	F
D	U	R	S	N	E	B	U	U	N	U	S	S	N
I	T	S	M	D	V	E	E	F	R	A	K	E	O
A	A	E	D	E	U	M	S	F	S	C	I	L	N
M	N	S	U	R	L	E	T	T	D	N	I	W	E
O	T	S	C	H	G	T	O	O	U	U	S	A	S
N	E	T	H	E	A	S	C	L	E	S	N	L	U
D	I	A	E	A	R	I	K	D	K	E	I	F	C
E	F	G	S	D	U	D	I	F	U	O	L	R	H
U	C	E	S	N	S	O	N	E	D	S	U	M	E
U	F	A	C	E	R	M	G	E	U	D	R	S	K

Answers

The Secret Language of Fan Flirting

Hold fan in front of the face with the left hand – I'd like to get to know you better, come and talk to me.

Hold fan in front of the face with the right hand – I'm off to the lemonade table for some refreshment, please follow my lead.

Twirl fan in right hand – I'm terribly sorry but my heart belongs to another.

Hold fan near to left ear – I'd really rather you placed your attentions elsewhere.

Carry fan in right hand – You seem a little too eager for my liking.

Gaze at closed fan – You seem to have misunderstood me.

Close the fan extremely slowly – I betroth myself to you and promise to be your wife.

Draw fan across the cheek – My heart is in your hands.

Twirl fan in the left hand – Please be aware that my chaperone is keeping a watchful eye on me.

Let the fan rest on right cheek – Yes.

Let the fan rest on left cheek – No.

Draw fan through the hand – Your behaviour towards me is somewhat vulgar.

Present shut – What are your true feelings towards me?

Draw fan across the eyes – Please forgive my dalliance.

Touch fan with the tip of finger – You are permitted to come and talk to me.

Open and shut – You are nothing but a rake and I know it.

Drop the fan – We will be friends.

Fan slowly – I am already married.

Fan quickly – I am betrothed to someone else.

Place handle of fan to the lips – You have permission to kiss me.

Hold fan wide open – I'm currently occupied with an utter bore but please don't take your leave just yet.

Place fan behind head – I think you're most becoming and you've caught my eye, please request an introduction.

Hanky Panky
The secret language of handkerchief flirting

Draw across the cheek – You have my heart.

Draw across the eyes – I'm sorry, please forgive me.

Draw across the forehead – My chaperone is near.

Draw through the hands – You disgust me!

Draw across the lips – I'd like to be introduced to you.

Fold – I'd like to speak with you.

Put in the pocket – I've no love to offer you at this time.

Twist in the right hand – My heart belongs to another.

Wind around the forefinger – I'm engaged.

Wind around the third finger – I'm married.

Mixed Messages

(a) Anthony Bridgerton

(b) Anthony Bridgerton

(c) Anthony Bridgerton

(d) Daphne Bridgerton

(e) Daphne Bridgerton

(f) Daphne Bridgerton

(g) Daphne Bridgerton

(h) Daphne Bridgerton

(i) Simon Basset

(j) Simon Basset

(k) Cressida Cowper

(l) Cressida Cowper

(m) Penelope Featherington

(n) Penelope Featherington

(o) Eloise Bridgerton

(p) Eloise Bridgerton

(q) Lady Danbury

(r) Lady Danbury

(s) Lady Danbury

(t) Lady Bridgerton

(u) Mrs Featherington

(v) Mrs Featherington

(w) Madame Delacroix

(x) Benedict Bridgerton

(y) Colin Bridgerton

(z) Marina Thompson

Glossary

O	U	I	N	O	O	W	S	F	U	T	H	E	I
H	D	C	N	T	V	I	S	C	O	U	N	T	S
C	E	O	S	D	W	N	B	S	T	W	W	T	N
R	B	U	B	U	E	O	L	N	O	N	S	S	F
D	U	R	S	N	E	B	U	U	N	U	S	S	N
I	T	S	M	D	V	E	E	F	R	A	K	E	O
A	A	E	D	E	U	M	S	F	S	C	I	L	N
M	N	S	U	R	L	E	T	T	D	N	I	W	E
O	T	S	C	H	G	T	O	O	U	U	S	A	S
N	E	T	H	E	A	S	C	L	E	S	N	L	U
D	I	A	E	A	R	I	K	D	K	E	I	F	C
E	F	G	S	D	U	D	I	F	U	O	L	R	H
U	C	E	S	N	S	O	N	E	D	S	U	M	E
U	F	A	C	E	R	M	G	E	U	D	R	S	K

Charlotte Browne

is an author and writer and has worked as a journalist
for a number of publications, from *The Independent*
to *Prima*. She has written for a variety of organisa-
tions within the non-profit and charity sector,
as well as adult and children's books.
She lives in South London.